OUT OF TOWN

---

40 GREAT WALKS
in the
NORTH of ENGLAND

Written by
ERIC ROBSON

Researcher
DAVID POWELL-THOMPSON

These walks were filmed as part of various television series produced for
Tyne Tees Television, Granada Television and Border Television.

Eric Robson only had to get himself and the dog to the top of the hill
whereas the long suffering camera crew had to flog to the top carrying
heavy backpacks of equipment.
The publishers would therefore like to express their thanks to
cameraman JANUSZ OSTROWSKI and sound recordist TERRY BLACK
in the hope that, having had their names in print,
they'll complain less next time.

ARENA PRESS
is a division of
ARENA BROADCAST

First Edition April 2002

A catalogue record for this book is available from The British Library.
British Library Cataloguing in Publication Data.

Cover photographs © Bill Guest

Designed by Ian Scott Design

Printed and bound by Spectrum Print, Cleethorpes

The contents of this publication are believed to be
correct at time of going to press but changes to routes do occur for all sorts of reasons.
The information given is intended only as a general guide and anyone following these
walks should carefully check their route with the relevant Ordnance Survey map
referred to in the text.

Walking, particularly in mountain areas, can be strenuous and the
weather unpredictable.
Individuals should ensure that they have suitable clothing, footwear,
provisions and maps.

On longer walks in remote areas walkers who plan to do the routes alone should let
someone know of their itinerary and at what time they expect to finish the walk.

Published by
ARENA PRESS
CRAG HOUSE FARM
WASDALE
CUMBRIA
CA19 1UT

ISBN   0 946812 02 0

CONTENTS

Introduction

Most walking books are boredom on legs. "Turn left at the green gate, cross three fields, mind the puddles and, (if you're not already asleep), follow the path downhill to ye Olde Tea Shoppe in the valley." They're about as exciting as the Darlington telephone directory and with nowhere near as good a cast list. If you've any sense you gave up buying them years ago.

What makes this collection of forty great walks in the North of England something else is that it's compiled by a cantankerous old cynic who looks at the world from a refreshingly different perspective. Often funny, frequently critical and sometimes downright offensive, he drags us Out of Town and introduces us to hidden treasures and secret byways in the North of England. He refuses to talk down to his readers, working instead on the principle that if they haven't got a nose for the maps and diagrams they shouldn't be let out on their own. You'll have to put up with his whims and prejudices about everything from dogs that wear waterproof jackets to officers of the Nanny State but he assumes you share them. He doesn't suffer fools gladly which makes it all the more surprising that he's done these walks with an ageing, bearded, chappie called Robson who's reasonably good company so long as he keeps his mouth shut, makes up for his deficiencies by being a passable chauffeur and carries lunch. Any walks that you don't like in this book are probably ones that he picked.

Now let's get on with it.

Gerard's Pennine Glen

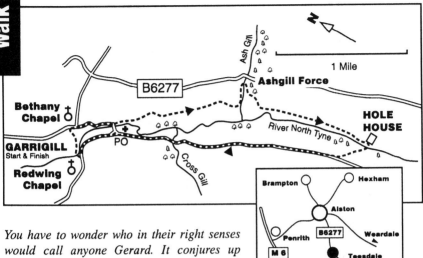

You have to wonder who in their right senses would call anyone Gerard. It conjures up images of nerds with pens in their top pocket and dandruffy partings. But, in a vain attempt to hang on to any Gerards who happen to have bought this book, let me say it was not always so. The Gerard we're talking about was a Saxon Chief. (He probably still had dandruff, but then all Saxons had dandruff because Helmet and Breastplate shampoo hadn't been invented.) Anyhow, this particular Chief Gerard apparently used to pop across from the Eden Valley with his flocks of sheep to pasture them each summer in the foothills of the Pennines, in a place named after him and which we know today as Garrigill. How it got from Gerard to Garrigill you'll have to ask someone a great deal cleverer than me.

5.25 Miles circular walk, boggy in parts with a couple of steepish climbs. 3 Hours.

The whole route is on OS Explorer OL31 North Pennines, Teesdale and Weardale starting and finishing at Map Reference NY745416.

Additional information is available in brochures which you can get from the enterprising little Post Office in Garrigill (which also sells cups of coffee and dog biscuits).

Start in the village churchyard where you'll find the grave of Westgarth Forster, Garrigill's most famous resident and the man who revolutionised the world of mining by writing the first definitive work on the strata of rocks. (It's the big flat grave slab in the middle). Now this chap may matter less to you than he did to the lead miners of Garrigill but the bearded one is into local history and insists that he's included.

If he's meddling at this stage of the proceedings it's a bad sign.

Wander out to the little broken chapel of Redwing where mining families gathered by the light of guttering tallow candles to practise an austere Methodism. Don't leave it too long before you visit because, judging by the state of the roof, the building isn't going to be with us much longer. Look through a crack in one of the boarded windows and you'll see the tiny, primitive reading desk and dusty, cramped box pews. Now, it may have been stern and straight laced in chapel but the village also supported at least two thriving pubs so there was obviously an element of pragmatism in Garrigill's Methodism as well.

Across the valley from Redwing (past what has to be the ugliest cricket pavilion this side of Karachi) there's another, grander chapel above the falls at Thortergill. On the climb out from there and along the fell breast there are wide views over field patterns and scattered farmsteads and the scars of dozens of little mines spread across the low Pennine hills. We're walking through a primitive Welfare State, past the remains of smallholdings rented out by the lead companies to the hard rock miners to allow them to keep a few sheep and hens and grow some of their food. It was also a crafty way of keeping the wages down.

The miners were great poachers. They probably had to be if they were going to stay on the right side of starvation. It's said that shortly after the Battle of Waterloo a local landowner brought in a detachment of Hussars to sort out the fly by nights who were lifting his pheasant and grouse. The poachers led the Hussars a merry dance across these hills and in and out of deep cut ravines until, eventually, they disappeared into the darkness of one of the mine levels. The Hussars were too frightened to follow. They may have been fine and dandy sorting out the French at Waterloo but the men of Garrigill, driven by hungry wives rather than delusions of empire, were more than a match for them.

We drop in to Ashgill which is the most attractive factory floor I've been to for many a long year. In this wooded cleft in the hills there are remains of stone bays where lead ore used to be stored before it was sorted and washed in the beck. There's the entrance to the Ashgill Horse Level which opened up one of the richest veins of lead in the area. And, providing the power and the glory in this industrial landscape, there's Ashgill Force. Made to look even more impressive by the soaring bridge arch above it, the water leaps from a broken ledge of rock one hundred feet to the boulder - strewn valley floor. Better still, you can pick your way through the haze of spray to a ledge behind the waterfall and look out through a slow motion wall of water to a woodland scene so magical that if King Arthur and his Knights of the Round Table rode up through the trees they wouldn't seem out of place.

At this point The Beard was taken away and made to lie down in a darkened room until the myths and legends wore off.

Ravenglass to Muncaster Fell

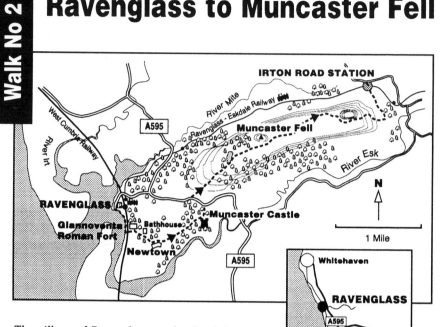

The village of Ravenglass on the Cumbrian coast was cleverly situated to ensure that it flooded whenever there was a high tide. After about 1800 years of wet feet they got round to putting a gate on the main street to keep the sea out. Cumbrians don't rush into things. But apparently it was Welsh speaking Celts who first established the place. Beard says that Yr Afon Glass means the town by the green river in Welsh and presumably described what the floors of most of the houses in the village looked like for part of the year.

---

6 mile walk returning to Ravenglass on the Ratty narrow gauge Railway. A long grunt out onto Muncaster Fell and an over the ankles boggy descent into Eskdale.

3 Hours plus additional time to visit Muncaster Castle and wait for the train at Irton Road.

The route is on OS Explorer OL6 The English Lakes South West starting and finishing at map reference SD085965

From the Ratty car park we stroll through the village and out onto the sands of the Ravenglass estuary. It was here in AD 79 that the Roman Governor Agricola moored a naval squadron – part of the expeditionary force that he hoped would eventually subdue the wild peoples of the North. Better men than him have tried. They started to build the fort of Glanaventa but omitted to tell the Ordnance Survey how to spell it. For some reason - perhaps planning restrictionarii - they picked a site between the United Utilities water pumping station and Railtrack's rickety Cumbrian Coastal Railway.

But in the glory days of an Empire that stretched as far as North Africa and deep into Eastern Europe Glanaventa was one of its most remote outposts. From this quartermaster's stores on the edge of the civilised world pack trains of horses would supply the Lakeland forts on Hardknott Pass and at Ambleside.

Through the trees are the remains of the Roman bath house. Now, credit where credit's due, the Romans were clever enough to invent the bath. And what fun bath night must have been with fifteen or twenty people sitting around in the suds chatting and scraping their skin clean. What's less well publicised is that they only ever emptied those baths a couple of times a year which is probably why washing didn't catch on in Britain for several centuries until carbolic soap and disinfectant were invented.

Scratching quietly we head out over the hill from Newton through a freshening breeze and widening views of the spectacular crowd of mountains at the head of the Eskdale Valley until the path drops through mature woodland into the grounds of Muncaster Castle.

The site of the castle, high above the winding River Mite has been occupied since Roman times but the Penningtons who own the place are Johnny-come-latelys having only been here since about 1200. (And he doesn't mean lunchtime.) The castle was renovated and made to look more quirkily mediaeval in the nineteenth century by the architect Salvin who also worked on Windsor Castle and the Tower of

London. Among the visitor attractions that used to be at Muncaster were a macaw that told the visitors to eff off and a family of bears that used to chase them down the back drive. It's friendlier, if less idiosyncratic, today.

On the hill opposite is a strange grey tower called Chapels that was built as a folly in the eighteenth century to mark the spot where a Muncaster shepherd met the castle's most famous visitor. During the Wars of the Roses King Henry VI was on the run after the battle of Hexham – no change there then. The Penningtons gave him shelter and when he ran off somewhere else he left his glass drinking bowl saying that so long as it remained intact the Penningtons would always thrive. It became known as The Luck of Muncaster and, very sensibly, it's kept in a padded box in a bank vault. By the way there's no truth in the story that the Penningtons, in return, gave the King a map of notable oak trees that he could hide in up and down his realm.

Past Muncaster Tarn where the estate has been fighting to keep back that Lakeland horticultural Triffid - Rhododendron Ponticum we climb out to the summit of Muncaster Fell. Behind us the sea and views of the Isle of Man on clear days. Ahead Hardknott Pass and the mountains of central Lakeland. But that's a walk for another, more energetic day. We're heading down to Irton Road Station to join the Ravenglass and Eskdale Railway which, unlike Railtrack, seems to be able to cope with the wrong sort of leaves and the wrong sort of weather. It's also run by amateurs.....

Yes, but what makes in different from the main line railway?

Brimham Rocks

This walk begins 300 million years ago, just before Beardy was born, when rivers flowing out of Scandinavia brought down deposits of coarse sand which they got sick of carrying by the time they reached Pateley Bridge. They created sand banks a mile and a half deep which were compressed then lifted by geological upheaval and weathered by scouring northern winds. I didn't catch you skip reading by any chance? Anyhow, what we're left with is a landscape where Dr. Dolittle meets Jurassic Park.

An easy 2 mile circular walk which you could do in an hour but I bet you'll spend longer working out the shapes of the stones.

Route on OS Explorer 298 Nidderdale, Fountains Abbey, Ripon and Pateley Bridge.

Plan of the stones from National Trust Visitor Centre.

At Brimham Rocks you can go on a fossilised big game hunt in the hills, following winding pathways through rock towers contorted into the shapes of fantastical beasts.

The Victorians, like the Romans, were very clever people. We know that because they told us so. At Brimham there was a particularly clever chap called Major Rook who was convinced that the extraordinary shapes he found there were man made. He'd seen Stonehenge and thought that some Druid sect or other had been at work here as well. Quite why the druids would have wanted to carve turtles and sphinxes and rabbits he never fully explained. We know now that any Druid who came to Brimham was either lost or overdosing on eye of newt and leg of toad.

What wind and weather have created here are crown and eagle, yoke of oxen and dancing bear, ET and a magic mushroom and even a vast ship of stone that rocks at anchor on a fossilised sea.

But the real fun of Brimham Rocks is to spot the statues that don't appear in the guide – the smiling rhinoceros and the elephant with its feet in the air; a grand piano and the dancing striptease artist (she's not dancing on the piano you understand); the 1930s radio and Tony Blair's smile; Bob the builder and a border terrier. OK, that last one is a flight of fancy too far.

Why? I spotted a decrepit old reporter on a string being led through the rocks by his canine carer but we didn't write that off as a flight of fancy too far.

The Wastwater Boulder Field

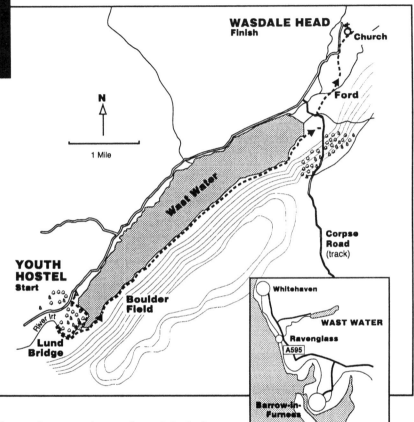

If your legs are shorter than eight inches or you've just spent three weeks rebuilding the rockery in your garden this is a walk to be avoided.

A fairly strenuous 6 mile walk at the end of which you'll need to be collected from the bar of the Wasdale Head Inn. Teetotallers can be collected, wet, from outside the Wasdale Head Inn

Route on OS Explorer OL6 The English Lakes South West starting at map reference NY144043

We're walking through the most atmospheric and brooding valley in the whole of the Lake District. It's a place that's driven people mad. Why he's maniacally muttering "present company excepted" I'm not sure.

The short walk in from the Wasdale Youth Hostel brings us to one of the Great British Views. The lake lapping quietly on a pebbled shore and stretching away to the foot of England's grandest mountains – Scafell and Great Gable flanked by their lieutenants Kirk Fell and Illgill Head. And on our right a fearsome wall of decaying rock that plunges into England's deepest lake and a dark chaos of rocks on the bottom 60 feet below sea level.

These are the Wastwater Screes which in an hour or so we'll have got to know rather better.

Most visitors to Lakeland, linked as they are by some invisible umbilical cord to their car, only ever see the Screes from the valley road which becomes a linear car park on bank holiday weekends. Hardier souls head off across Irton Pike and Whin Rigg and Illgill Head to look down the yawning chasms of the Screes from the top. But we're going to get a fresh perspective by climbing across the moonscape of boulders along the waterline.

It starts with a woodland walk through dappled shade along the River Irt but it soon changes to something much more exciting.

("Exciting" is the bearded one's description. By the time I'd disappeared into the twentieth crevasse, "stupid" was a word that sprang more readily to mind.)

It's hard going in parts as you try to identify paths across the boulder field. You'll find yourself concentrating so hard on your toe ends that you inadvertently get higher on the slope and, every so often, come to tongues of loose scree with scarcely a foothold between you and the water fifty or sixty feet below. Some of the rocks you have to negotiate are the size of small cars. Other parts of the slope are a jumble of smaller stones that rock and slide unnervingly as you put your weight on them.

And then you're through it onto an undulating, grassy track heading for the finest valley head in Britain. Ahead there's a pattern of tiny stone walled fields tucked away into the shadows of an amphitheatre of mountains.

We pass the Corpse Road across which the dead of Wasdale were taken across a mountain pass into Eskdale for burial and visit what's said to be England's smallest church – St Olaf's at Wasdale Head. We could also tell you about the creature - part wolf, part fox that terrorised these valleys and the story of the man from Wasdale Head who lived in a turnip. But when you hear that Wasdale is home of the competition to find the world's biggest liar you probably wouldn't believe us.

Monsal Trail

N
↑

⌐ ‾ ‾ ‾ ‾ ‾ ‾ ‾ ‾ ⌐
└ ‾ ‾ ‾ ‾ ‾ ‾ ‾ ‾ ┘ Dismantled Railway Bed

1 Mile

Millers Dale

Litton
Mill

Cressbrook Mill

Water-cum-Jolly Dale

Long Lane

A6

River Wye

Finish TADDINGTON

Start
MONSAL
HEAD

P

Manchester   Sheffield
Chesterfield

Buxton

MONSAL
HEAD   Matlock   M1

M6

A6

Stoke

Derby

Child labour and brutality are the themes of this little walk in the White Peak. Beardo certainly knows how to show a chap a good time.

A gentle 5 mile linear walk in which the brutality is all in the stories. It should take you about 3 hours returning from Taddington by bus.

For bus service details ring 0870 6082608

Route on OS Explorer OL 24 – White Peak starting at map reference SK185715 and ending at SK136713.

From Monsal Head in Derbyshire we drop in to a viewpoint above the beautiful valley of the River Wye – a viaduct on what was once the Midland Main Line from London St Pancras to Manchester. Behind us there's the blackened and barred mouth of one of the echoing railway tunnels.

In the same way that William Wordsworth objected to the coming of the railways in Lakeland, here it was John Ruskin who got his pen in a lather about the evils of the iron horse.

"There was a rocky valley between Buxton and Bakewell. You might have seen the Gods there morning and evening. Apollo and all the sweet muses of the light walking in fair procession on the lawns of it. You enterprised a railway through that valley. You blasted its rocks away. You heaped thousands of tons of shale into its lovely stream. The valley has gone and the Gods with it." He wasn't a happy man.

But all you needed was patience, Mr Ruskin. Nature is reclaiming the valley for its own, the railway is gone and we're walking in fair procession along the overgrown track bed of it. As sunlight dances through the birch trees it's as if Apollo and the muses are back.....

Carry on walking on your own for a few minutes while I take the beard to one side and give him his tablets. Thank you.

....as the light changes so the spirits of Ruskin's gentler vision fade. Another blocked tunnel forces us away from the line of the railway and down a long incline across the hill. Suddenly we're in a different world of brooding mills glowering through the trees. There's Cressbrook Mill owned by Arkwright the cotton king. Under high limestone cliffs we skirt a mill pond in a verdant valley with the cheery name of Water Cum Jolly Dale. It wouldn't have been very jolly for the sweated labourers who walked this way to work. And then round a bend in the river we come to a place that was the dark underworld of the industrial revolution. Litton Mill is a bleak ruin surrounded by thickets of wild raspberries and blackberries where its workers would have scavenged for food. It had a terrible reputation as an exploiter of child labour. Its owners would buy what they called apprentices from workhouses in places like Bethnal Green and bring them here to a life of starvation and slavery. So many children died here that their bodies were shipped out for burial in neighbouring parishes so that people wouldn't realise how bad the conditions were.

It's a vale of tears even today. With a shudder we turn our backs on it and walk away down Millers Dale. It's a place you won't forget.

Wallington to Belsay

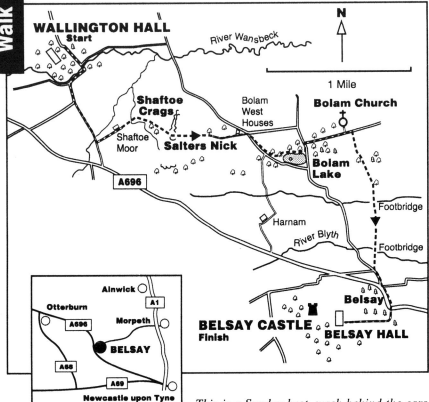

This is a Sunday best, wash behind the ears and trim the beard sort of walk because we're in smart company. *Scruffy terriers are, however, permitted because the Northumbrian gentry always appreciated a mad ratter.*

NOTE: For those readers who aren't related to the Northumbrian gentry. A mad ratter is a dog that's particularly good at hunting rats. It shouldn't be confused with a mad hatter, at least one of which can be found in the pedigree of most Northumbrian aristocratic families.

Wallington Hall was the happy hunting ground of the Fenwicks, the Blacketts and the Trevelyans. The Fenwicks and the Blacketts made the brass. It's said that the griffons on the front lawn of Wallington originally came from London's Bishopsgate which was being demolished in the name of development and progress. They were brought to the North East of England as ballast in coal ships owned by the Blacketts.

The Trevelyans were a different deal altogether. They were cultured – and turned the place into a madhouse of artists and writers. No wonder they ended up having to give it to The National Trust.

Before you set out down the route take an hour to visit the Wallington walled gardens which are an object lesson in how to translate the glories of a disappeared age into an understandable modern form.

We wander through mature parkland and across an utterly impractical but perfectly proportioned bridge over the River Wansbeck. These were tamed landscapes, titivated by the 18th century equivalent of Dimmock and Titchmarsh – style gurus like Capability Brown who was born just down the road at Kirkharle. They were makeover merchants on a grand scale. It took them longer than a frantically filmed weekend to do the business but the outcome was rather the same. The scruffy turned into the fashionable as quickly as possible. Only the chequebook was troubled. And at least in the eighteenth century blue decking hadn't been invented.

Drifts of radiant gorse line the pack horse track out onto the hill as we aim for the deep cleft of Salter's Nick through Shaftoe Crags on the skyline. In the eye of the eighteenth century landscape improvers rocky outcrops like these were a blessing. Here was nature in all its horror but just far enough away from the house that the ladies wouldn't come over all faint at the sight of it.

Beard is muttering about how much he dislikes Culpability Brown and all his works as we walk down to the gentler reaches of Bolam Lake.

The first sight of the mansion of Belsay is extraordinary. Out of the Northumbrian countryside rears a structure designed in such Doric brutality that it could have come from the drawing board of Albert Speer. Its proportions may be impeccable, its embodiment of classical themes superlative but it's a frightening house. It broods with delusions of grandeur and threats of the abuse of power.

We take refuge in a hole in the ground. A deep ravine invites us into the hillside. It's from here that the stone for the house was quarried. And it's here that they created Belsay's greatest triumph – the quarry garden. Paths meander among towering walls of rock and under high stone arches and pinnacles all softened by exotic trees and shrubs and tumbling ivy. And there's another bonus. You can't see the house from here.

But it's in this secret world that the Middleton's of Belsay Hall would have kept their hermit. Hermit keeping was very fashionable in the late eighteenth century. Advertisements setting out terms and conditions could be found in the Hermits Wanted column of the Gentleman's Magazine. Once appointed the hermit would be expected to live in some garden grotto where he would be on display when visitors came. He wouldn't be allowed to cut his hair or nails and he'd be dressed in a coat of rags which had probably been run up by the lady of the house's dressmaker. He was the ultimate garden accessory.

The arrangement didn't always work out. On one estate where the hermit had been engaged for seven years, after three months he was found sloping off to the local pub. But another landowner found the ultimate solution to problems of hermit labour relations. Sir Richard Hill of Hawkstone had his hermit stuffed.

Penshaw

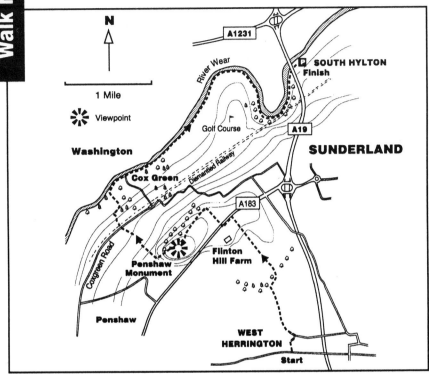

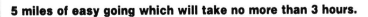

He's finally gone mad.

We're to meet up at a cemetery in West Herrington just off the A19. And, with the greatest respect to the good residents of West Herrington, it has as much chance of being designated an Area of Outstanding Natural Beauty as Wallsend or Warrington.

And in just two sentences the beard has got up the noses of three northern communities.

---

5 miles of easy going which will take no more than 3 hours.

Route on OS Explorer 308 Durham and Sunderland starting at map reference NZ347530 and finishing at NZ350568

West Herrington is the sort of place where town and country smack each other in the mouth, but just a couple of hundred yards into the walk we're in a different world. It could be one of those genteel Northumbrian landscapes that we found near Wallington as we head for the folly on the hill.

The first time I visited Penshaw Monument was with that great Bishop of Durham and scourge of the tabloid press David Jenkins. When he first got the job and when the papers were full of those stories of thunderbolts from heaven burning down York Minister to protest at the ordination there of a Godless Bishop a colleague brought him up here. He said it was like Moses on Mount Pisgah looking out on the Promised Land. You can see from Durham Cathedral to the Angel of the North. Stretching away below him were the challenges that his new job was going to bring – fading industry and rampant unemployment; poverty and division. Theological niceties about how many angels can balance on the head of a riveter's hammer and five dodgy translations of the phrase Virgin Birth were suddenly set in a more robust context. (To continue this line of argument read Beard's other book – 50 Walks Through Biblical History, remaindered in a bookshop near you.) But, in the meantime, can we get on with the walk?

We climb the hill with the vast stone pillars of the Temple of Theseus towering over us and step onto a piazza in the sky. There's a fair chance of stepping on a pizza in the sky as well because Penshaw is not a litter free zone.

The Penshaw Monument was built by public subscription in 1844 to the memory of John George Lambton, First Earl of Durham. He was better known as Radical Jack, author of the First Reform Bill. He had a full life. He was also Lord Privy Seal, Ambassador Extraordinary and Governor of Canada and by the time he was my age he'd been dead for five years. Puts us all to shame.

Over our shoulder the monument will dominate the horizon for the rest of the walk, catching the shifting light, becoming more ethereal as it melts into the grey distance.

We come down to the River Wear at the village of Cox Green which used to be a thriving port and shipyard until the middle of the nineteenth century. Now they dismantle ships on the mudflats. But out along the sweeping bends in the river the landscape hasn't changed a great deal since Radical Jack's day. Wooded cliffs stand high above the water on one bank, wide rolling fields of grain and oil seed stretch away on the other. There are little farms tucked in by the riverbank. All just three or four miles from the centre of Sunderland.

And then the nineteenth century runs head on into the twenty first. Above the path rears the A19 flyover, its concrete slab walls ornamented with the angry graffiti of the brave new world. Come back Radical Jack. Your talents are needed now more than ever.

Old Bewick

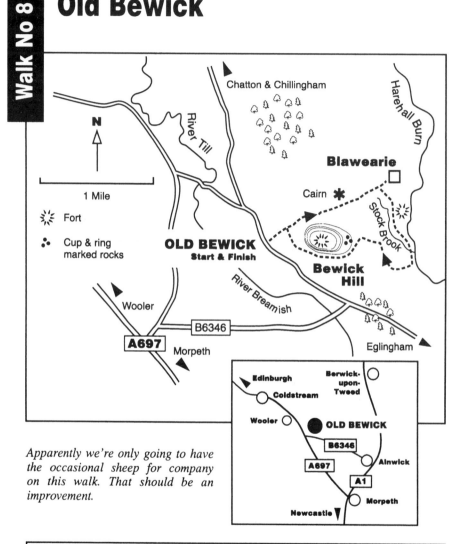

Apparently we're only going to have the occasional sheep for company on this walk. That should be an improvement.

4 easy miles with just one climb out onto Bewick Hill. 2 hours plus exploration time.

Route on OS Explorer 332 Alnwick and Amble. Start and finish at map reference NU067215.

Bewick means the town of the bees but why it once had a reputation for bee keeping is a mystery. With the sweep of the Cheviots as a backdrop we're climbing out onto Bewick Hill. Deserted today it was part of one of the most dynamic communities in Northumberland four thousand years ago. There are remnants of forts and settlements on surrounding hills such as Yeavering Bell and ahead of us, in the middle of the moor, the piled stones of a great cairn. Its burial cysts and grave covers are still in place. When it was excavated in the 1860s they found the bodies of a mother and child together with jewellery and household utensils that were presumably put there to ease their journey into a prehistoric spirit world.

(Note from Beard Age Man's companion. Any reader not wanting to study for a PHD in ancient burial practices and the continuity of human settlement in a Northumbrian landscape should skip on to walk nine.)

And people lingered up here long after the Bronze Age faded. We arrive at the little derelict farm of Blawearie – the place where the wind always blows. Appropriate. Because one of the best preserved buildings in the old farm steading is a nettie with one of the best views in the north of England.

(Note for all readers who live south of the Humber or who have an avocado coloured bathroom suite or bidet – a nettie is an outside lavatory.)

Bewick Hill with its long views across the eastern Borders has been a place that people chose as a defensible site from prehistory to the Second World War. By Bewick Hill Fort there's a concrete pillbox with as good a view as the nettie. It must have been a canny billet for the Northumbrian equivalent of Capn. Mainwaring and his boys. They certainly wouldn't have been troubled much by Germans. Ghosts of Bronze Age warriors might have been more troublesome though.

Stupid boy.

And then on the way down from the hill we stumble across the genuine

Ripon to Fountains Abbey

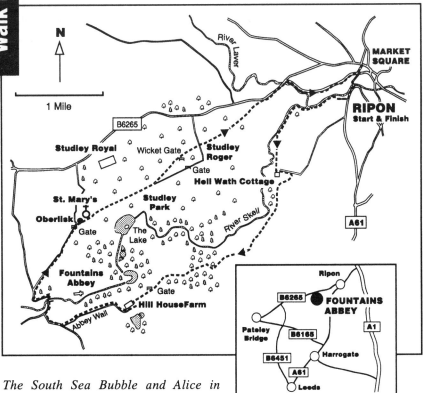

The South Sea Bubble and Alice in Wonderland are the two bits of nonsense greybeard promises on this walk. Personally I'm hoping for an encounter with the Cheshire cat.

---

8 miles circular walk with a few strenuous bits. It should take you about 4 hours plus time to explore Ripon, Fountains Abbey and Studley Royal.

Route on OS Explorer 298 Nidderdale starting and finishing at map reference SE312713.

Details of opening hours at Fountains Abbey and Studley Royal from The National Trust on 01765 608888

A slim volume picked up from a newsagent in Ripon started us off on the trail of Alice in Wonderland and other strange creations. It said, with a boldness that belied its status as a mere pamphlet, *"It's generally accepted that after The Bible and Shakespeare Lewis Carroll is the greatest influence on the English language."* Really. I'm sure that Milton and Wordsworth and Thomas Hardy might have a thing or two to say about that. But what I suspect the pamphlet's authors were building up to is that Alice and her creator have been ever so helpful to the Ripon tourist industry. The real Lewis Carroll - Charles Lutwidge Dodgson, was the son of a Canon at Ripon Minster. It was from carvings in the Cathedral that he drew the inspiration for characters such as the Bellman, the rabbit disappearing into its burrow and the elephant balanced on a turtle's back.

We set off through long tunnels of hawthorn along the River Skell to hunt not for the Snark but for gentle walking into a gracious past. I glanced across at the dog and saw that this time it vanished quite slowly, beginning with the end of the tail and ending with the grin which remained for some time after the rest of it had gone. Wishful thinking, I fear.

It has to be the ultimate insult comparing a border terrier to some inanely grinning cat. But you are old Father William the young dog said, and your hair has become very white.

Truce.

You have to imagine that it's the year 1132. We're in the company of a little group of bedraggled monks who've fallen out with the powers that be at the Benedictine House of St. Mary's in York. They thought that life was too soft there. To be true to the Rule of St Benedict they were looking for what they described as their desert in the north. They found it in this damp and rocky valley three miles from Ripon – *"a place more fit for wild beasts than men to inhabit."* Here they laid the spiritual foundations of Fountains Abbey.

Ironically, from those simple beginnings the Abbey became one of the wealthiest religious houses in England. The wealth came from wool. Fountains sheep flocks were grazed on estates that stretched as far as the Lake District and Teesside.

Today it's a ruin in the mist but if you lean over the Abbey wall you can almost hear the plainsong echoes of 900 years ago.

The next mile of bridleway is a time machine that transports us from the twelfth to the eighteenth century.

The ruins were bought as a picturesque addition to the landscaped Studley Royal Estate which had been created by a character that could have graced a Lewis Carroll nonsense poem except you'd have thought he was too far fetched. John Aislaby was the Tory Member of Parliament for Ripon until he saw the way the wind was blowing, changed sides and became Chancellor of the Exchequer in the Whig administration of 1718. In a list with many candidates he was probably one of the worst Chancellors ever. He was also the promoter of something called The South Sea Company Scheme. When that dodgy financial venture collapsed in what became known as the South Sea Bubble he was kicked out of Parliament and banned from public office for life.

In a lesson that's been well learned by the directors of so many high profile failed companies ever since, he managed to keep enough of his personal fortune intact to be able to remodel half of Yorkshire. Never mind the shareholders, build a Palladian temple or two.

It's a lovely walk through the deer park to the old estate village of Studley Roger on the way back to Ripon. There aren't many people about to hear us muttering as we go about the iniquities of power and patronage.

It was the shout of "Come the Revolution" echoing through the trees and almost frightening an old lady off her bike that persuaded me it was about time I whisked him away.

High Peak

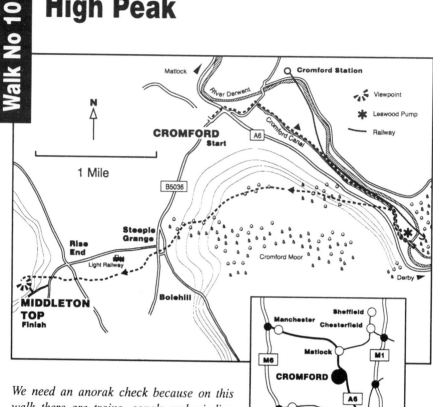

We need an anorak check because on this walk there are trains, canals and winding engines. Anyone who's stood on the end of a platform at Crewe station with a camcorder videoing carriages on Virgin Trains join the group on the left. The rest of you can come with us.

A 5 mile linear walk that should take about 3 hours.

There are two long ascents but it's no use waiting for the train because service was suspended 40 years ago.

Route on OS Explorer OL 24 The Peak District White Peak area starting at map reference SK296569 and finishing at SK275551.

Details of the running of the Leawood Pump and Middleton Top Engine from 01629 823204

It starts as an effortless stroll along one of the prettiest towpaths in Britain. We're walking alongside the Cromford Canal in Derbyshire. Little Grebes nest amongst the water lilies. Elder and Hawthorn shade the path. And everywhere you look there are the remains of what was, once, a busy commercial waterway. Aqueducts and canalside warehouses and silted locks. The grandest of all the buildings is the one that houses the steam driven Leawood Pump that used to lift water from the River Derwent to top up the canal.

At Cromford Junction they planned the greatest engineering challenge of the canal age – the Cromford and High Peak which would carry freight thirty miles over the hill to Whaley Bridge. Unfortunately they couldn't find a supply of water to fill the cut on the top of the hill and so they decided to build a railway instead. It would take the same route with rope hauled wagonways replacing the flights of locks on gradients up to one in eight. It became the steepest railway in Britain.

As you will soon find out when you begin the long climb out of the valley. You could do the route the other way round – downhill all the way – but where's the challenge in that.

In the early days runaway wagons were a nuisance. On a number of occasions fully loaded trains went walkabout, going so fast by the time they reached the bottom of the incline at Cromford Junction that they cleared the canal. It must have been a spectacular sight if you were watching from a safe distance. To overcome the problem they built something called a catch pit into which the pointsman could divert runaway rolling stock. The last escapee is still in there.

We grunt our way to the plateau half way to Middleton Top where a bit of this rail network in the hills survives. It's the Killer Branch named not because of its safety record but after the Killer family who built it to haul limestone out of their quarries. Now it's run by enthusiasts. You can tell they're enthusiasts because when we arrive all that's to be seen of them is various sets of legs in oily overalls sticking out of the business end of a little green locomotive. The conversation (muffled because the heads are still in the machine) turns to 0-4-0s and steam pressure return valves. Which is odd because this particular locomotive is powered by a Fort Cortina engine. A knackered Ford Cortina engine as it happens. Our hopes of an exhilarating spin on the Killer evaporate.

All along the lineside of the Cromford and High Peak are the cliff faces of worked out quarries softened by shimmering birch and alive with echoing birdsong. Long views across the valley are dominated by the modern equivalent – the quarries that are still working their blasted ledges of limestone across the face of the hill.

A lone signal forever set at danger marks journey's end by the winding house at Middleton Top. We've been walking a railway that was part Victorian engineering excellence and part Heath Robinson inventiveness. When you stand dwarfed by the polished and painted flywheel of the Middleton winding engine that used to drag fully laden trains to this summit you'll perhaps agree that the most extraordinary thing of all about this line is that it kept working right up to 1963 when these magnificent machines finally fell silent.

I think I can spot a tear in beard's eye. Time to change his anorak and take him home for a lie down in a darkened room.

California, here we come

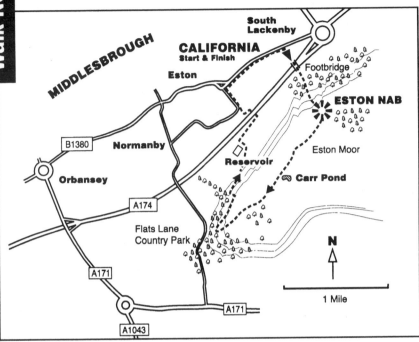

Don't get your hopes up. This is California Teesside rather than Stateside. But at least we won't have to share our route with the shrinks, counsellors, religious fundamentalists and food fanatics that seem to make up such a percentage of the population of the Sunshine State.

Maybe I should explain that my short, fat and hairy companion once had a bad experience with a Greyhound bus and has never been quite the same since. Now stop being xenophobic while I give these good people details of the route.

Pray, silence for the beardman of Alcatraz.

A 4 mile circular route with one stiff climb

Route on OS Explorer OL 26 North York Moors Western Area starting and finishing at map reference NZ558188

We're climbing out across a tree covered hillside onto Eston Nab – the hollow mountain. More than seven hundred miners laboured underground here, cutting away at one of the richest sources of ironstone in the north of England. It's said they took out sixty three million tons of the stuff, every ton hauled away by one of the two hundred or so horses that worked underground and were stabled at California down in the valley bottom.

Through a scrub of birch and hazel there's the sealed yellow brick arch of the mine entrance that would once have echoed to the accented voices of hard rock miners from as far afield as Norfolk and Cornwall who came here the year after the American gold rush to try to make a living in this northern Klondike. You can bet your life that none of them made a fortune.

A scramble through piles of rough and jumbled boulders above the old mine tramways and loading bays takes us onto the summit. There are distant views towards Roseberry Topping with its promise of bigger and more remote walks in the hills. But every bit as impressive is the panorama of industrial Teesside stretching away below us to the sea.

In a gentle breeze we wander out to a rough pillar built from the stone of a mine house to commemorate the workers of Eston Nab; to celebrate the wealth of raw materials that forged Teesside's industrial revolution. The memorial is dwarfed now by a mobile phone mast. There used to be a warning beacon here during the Napoleonic Wars and three and a half thousand years before that a bronze age camp. Ancient trackways and pack horse trails criss cross the summit. But on the day we visit we have the place entirely to ourselves. We take a high level stroll past Carr Pond before heading down to the back to back houses of California over a slope of rounded spoil heaps that advancing vegetation is doing its best to disguise.

Raq's star rating. **

A must for industrial archaeologists and people who want to be able to tell their mates in the pub that they went to California on their holidays.

Harsh. Very harsh.

The Wainstones

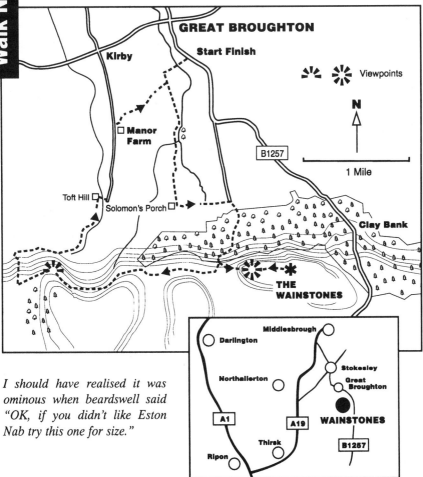

I should have realised it was ominous when beardswell said "OK, if you didn't like Eston Nab try this one for size."

A 6 mile circular walk with a bit of energetic climbing which should take about 3 hours except that in good weather I bet you spend an hour on the top enjoying the spectacular views.

Route on OS Explorer OL 26 North York Moors Western Area starting and finishing at NT548060

We're walking into the hills from the Cleveland Plain, aiming for a cathedral of fractured rock that's dominated the skyline most of the way from Great Broughton.

The climb on good paths takes us through moorland and conifer plantation to a high ridge of gentle walking. Before we get any short, fat, hairy legged complaints, yes, you can see distant Middlesbrough on this walk too but we're in wilder, higher country on the edge of the Cleveland Hills.

At the end of the ridge The Wainstones look like a natural, frost-riven formation but once they were quarried for stone to build the older houses of Great Broughton. What's left is a giant's playpen of building blocks balanced over narrow, winding tunnels. The highest of the slabs of rock provide an exposed and spectacular viewing platform from which you can look out across a carpet of patterned fields and villages in miniature,

There's some dispute about the name Wainstones. The local name for them is the windstones. Another theory says that the name comes from a Saxon word, wanean, meaning to howl. You can just imagine the sound they would make as they splintered an autumn gale.

And getting the retaliation in first, yes, there are spoil heaps on the broad track down from the Wainstones but these are the remains of a very different industry from the one we saw at Eston Nab. This was once the land of the jet miners. While we walk for the sheer pleasure and freedom of it they came this way six days a week through the confines of a working lifetime. The paths are beaten hard by generations of workers' clogs.

Jet is a form of lignite, a sort of fossilised wood. It's found sandwiched between deposits of ironstone and alum shales. From the fourteenth century it was thought to have magical properties. Crucifixes were carved from it in the belief that they would ward off evil spirits and moaning border terriers.

Sorry.

But the jet industry really came into its own because of Victorian funereal fashion. The gleaming black jet necklace was an essential mourning accessory for Victorian middle class ladies. So next time you put on your jet necklace spare a thought for the working men with calloused hands who won it from these exposed slopes of the Cleveland Hills.

You know, I never realised that he had a jet necklace. But I bet it sets off the greys of his beard ever so nicely.

The Arnside Bore

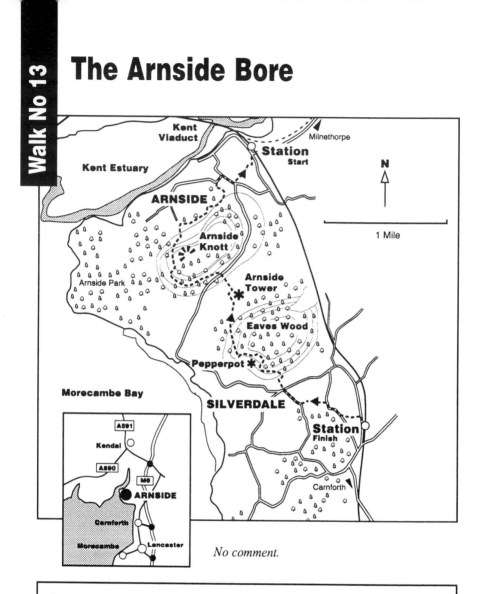

No comment.

A 4.25 mile linear walk returning by railway. At the start of the walk leave your car at Arnside station and take the train to Silverdale. 3 hours of easy walking.

Route on OS Explorer OL7 The English Lakes South Eastern Area starting at map reference SD476752 and finishing at map reference SD461788

The train chunters over the Kent viaduct into Arnside station and squeals to a halt. I've always thought that a train journey makes an exciting start to a day's walking. Not that this is much of a train journey – just three miles down the line to Silverdale. If more than half a dozen people get on at Arnside the guard has a struggle selling them all a ticket.

I'd read time and again what a beautiful place Silverdale is but I've got to say that the first sight of it is not hopeful. Unless you like bungalows and caravan parks. But then we walk out into Eaves Wood and can suddenly believe everything we've read in the guide books. It's an ancient coppiced woodland overlaid with a Victorian pleasure ground. Alongside the pathways there are the clints and grikes of limestone pavement that have escaped the depredations of rockery building vandals. It's a site of special scientific importance and a habitat for rare butterflies. I can't remember which and as I have great difficulty telling the difference between a purple edged fritillary and a greater buff bazoomber you'll have to rely on your own entomological skills.

We come out of the trees onto a clear, limestone summit at the edge of which is The Pepperpot, a rustic tower built up here in 1887 to commemorate Queen Victoria's Golden Jubilee. Perhaps its sponsors wouldn't have bothered if they'd known that the British nuclear industry was going to screw up the view across Morecambe sands by building the monstrous blocks of Heysham Nuclear Power Station in the middle of it.

Shaded pathways lead us down to the saddle between Eaves Wood and Arnside Knot and the ruins of Arnside Tower. It was a fortified house built as a bulwark against Scots invaders. Once a stronghold of the Stanleys, Earls of Derby it's now a nest box for crows and pigeons. It must have scared many a snoozing bird half to death the night in 1884 when a quarter of the tower fell down in a gale.

Ahead and above us is the steep limestone scree of Arnside Knot but you won't be expected to march up the front of it. The path meanders through the trees until we emerge onto a bare summit with one of the best views of the Lakeland mountains that you'll get anywhere. From Black Combe and Caw in the South West through the Skiddaw Range and The Langdales to the Helvellyn summits away to the north it's a spectacular panorama of the roof of England. On a clear day you can even see Skiddaw more than thirty miles away on the other side of the Lake District.

Below us are the sands of the Kent Estuary and the little town of Arnside. Which brings us to the bore. If your visit coincides with a particularly high tide you should be able to stand up here on Arnside Knot and watch what looks like a freak wave rush in from Morecambe Bay and crash between the piers of the railway viaduct that spans the River Kent. It happens a couple of hours before high water so you'll have to consult the tide tables. I said you should be able to stand up here and see it because that's the theory. Every time I've been to Arnside I've missed it.

As we wandered down to collect the beardmobile at Arnside Station my well meaning suggestions about bores and boredom fell on deaf ears.

I think I preferred "no comment."

Walking the Waverley

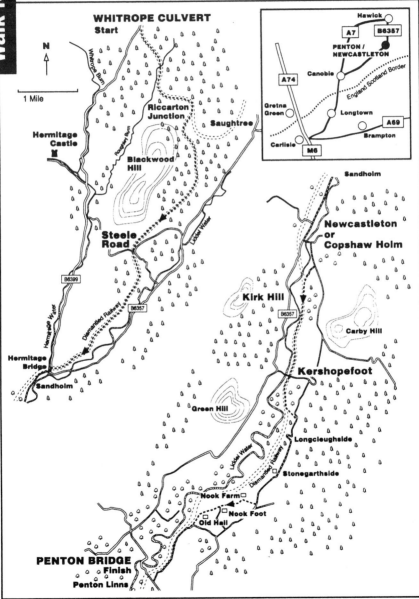

WHITROPE CULVERT
Start

N

1 Mile

Whitrope Burn

Hawick

A7   B6357

**PENTON /
NEWCASTLETON**

Canobie

A74

England Scotland Border

Gretna
Green

Longtown

A69

Carlisle   M6

Brampton

Riccarton
Junction

Saughtree

Hermitage
Castle

Rougive Burn

Blackwood
Hill

Sandholm

Steele
Road

Liddel Water

Newcastleton
or
Copshaw Holm

B6399

Hermitage Water

Dismantled Railway

B6357

Kirk Hill

B6357

Carby Hill

Hermitage
Bridge

Sandholm

Kershopefoot

Green Hill

Longcleughside

Liddel Water

Dismantled Railway

Stonegarthside

Nook Farm

Nook Foot

Old Hall

PENTON BRIDGE
Finish

Penton Linns

You've probably already spotted that the bearded wonder is drawn to railways like a moth to a candle flame. Just a flash of firebox or a whiff of steam and some primitive instinct has him transfixed. Once I thought there was the chance of a cure but when I found him wandering about pretending to sound like a banking engine on a railway that had been shut for almost fifty years it was obvious that, in this as in so many things, he was a hopeless case.

A 19 mile linear walk that will need a friendly driver to drop you at the start and pick you up with tea and sympathy at the end. It's a long way but it's easy walking and you can join the route almost anywhere along its length to do the bit you want.

Route on OS Explorer 324 Liddesdale and Kershope Forest starting at map reference NY525000 and finishing at map reference NY433774

If you were feeling really energetic you could walk the whole route of the Waverley Line – all ninety four and a half miles of it from Edinburgh to Carlisle.

Deafening silence.

OK, we'll work up to that.

The training starts here in the bleak, high country around Whitrope Summit. We're at the top of a fearsome and exposed stretch of railway that used to test the skills of locomotive firemen coaxing their engines up a one in seventy gradient from the Border town of Hawick. At Whitrope tunnel (now blocked off because of a roof fall) they could pause for breath as they started the long descent into England.

Rolling hills and wooded valleys stretch away from a trackbed that meanders through deep cuttings and across high, windswept embankments until we puff into Riccarton Junction. Here in the back of beyond there used to be a little community connected to the outside world only by railway. Births, deaths, marriages and groceries all relied on the train. Most of Riccarton was bulldozed by the Forestry

Commission after the line closed but on what remains of the derelict platform a group of railway enthusiasts have put up two new Riccarton Junction signs. Stark and incongruous it's as if they're waiting for the ghost train.

Further south into Liddesdale you'll find yourselves sharing part of the route with sheep and cattle. Local farmers have pressed the abandoned track into service as a handy place to feed their stock. And watch out for curly wires stretched at waist height across the line because they're electric fences.

Steaming round a shallow bend we wheeze to a halt at what used to be Newcastleton Station. It's hard to imagine it now but Newcastleton regularly won the prize for best kept station on the Waverley Line when my grandfather was station master here. And in that bramble thicket was a signal box where the young Robson used to watch the hauling of the levers and listen to the clacking of the telegraph that alerted the signalman to the progress of trains on the line....

Talk amongst yourselves while I try to shunt him out of memory lane.

In the corner of the signal box was a huge black wheel that the signalman used to let me wind to open the level crossing gates....

Yes, and you used to listen to Dan Dare on Radio Luxembourg and there was bread and jam for tea.

And at the level crossing we used to put old pennies on the track and press our noses against the gate to watch express trains crush them into metal pancakes.

And any moment now we're going to hear the music from the Hovis commercial and man and dog will walk off into a golden sunset.

But I digress. It was on the level crossing at Newcastleton in the 1960s that the Waverley line made its last stand. A group of protesters including the Church of Scotland Minister with his trumpet occupied the crossing and refused to allow the last train through. It made a brief news story but the line still closed. Trumpet playing clergymen are no match for tone deaf accountants.

South of Newcastleton the line skirts the remains of Mangerton, one of the Border Pele Towers that date from an age when Liddesdale was one of the most lawless places in Europe. The Armstrongs and Elliots held sway here. Border Reivers that thumbed their noses at the Governments of England and Scotland and murdered, robbed and ransomed for four bloody centuries. The Robsons are later imports. They still murdered, robbed and ransomed but from across the border in Tynedale.

On a bridge over the Kershope Burn we thunder into England and immediately the difference between walking rules north and south of the border is obvious. A rash of PRIVATE and KEEP OUT signs divert us from the line of the railway onto tracks and byways as we head for the last redundant station on our railway mystery tour. Penton is PRIVATE, too, but once it was the remote railhead for one of the most delightful riverscapes in the border country.

Fortunately one bank of the River Liddel at Penton Linns is in Scotland and, better still, is owned by one of the most progressive landlords in the country – Buccleuch Estates. As if to cock a snook at the privateers across the river they've put up a sign welcoming walkers. So we accept their invitation and walk into the wood. Within two hundred yards we're looking down on a geological masterpiece. Buckled rock strata fold upwards out of the river and disappear below the water again before the far bank. But the middle has been carved out by aeons of flash floods to leave a full bottom set of tectonic dentures. Through them pours a spate river boiling brown and cream like a mouth in time drinking the biggest glass of best bitter that's ever been invented.

At which point we abandon walking and head for the pub at Penton Bridge to wait for our lift. In the following hour Beard does a passable impersonation of the River Liddel and I get a bowl of water and half a packet of crisps. Fair, or what?

The Heights of Hong Kong

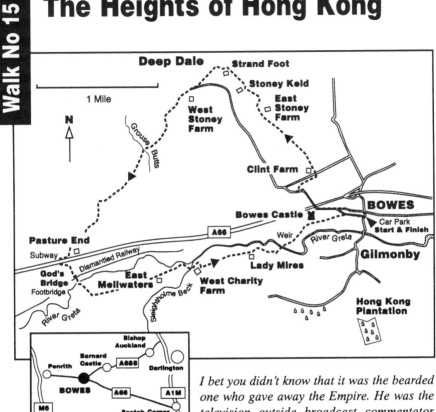

I bet you didn't know that it was the bearded one who gave away the Empire. He was the television outside broadcast commentator that day when Governor Chris Patten finally rolled up the flag, climbed aboard the Royal Yacht Britannia and, wiping away a tear, sailed off into the darkness leaving Hong Kong to the Chinese.

I bet you don't care either. But that's by the by. I only mention the fact to explain why we found ourselves in the mists of the North Pennines trying to find another Hong Kong which he'll presumably give away with similar gay abandon. The mystery is why the Chinese would want it given that the next nearest Chinese territory is a carry out in Penrith.

---

8 miles of easy wandering that should take you about 4 hours.

Route on OS Explorer OL 31 North Pennines, Teesdale and Weardale starting and finishing in Bowes at map reference NY996135

The dog's in a particularly bolshie frame of mind as we park up in Bowes. A taste of good old fashioned discipline is obviously what he needs. Which is why we're standing outside one of the most infamous schools in British literary history. It's said that Charles Dickens spent some time at a hotel in the town when he was writing Nicholas Nickleby. His inspiration for Dotheboys Hall, where the pupils were terrorised by headmaster Wackford Squeers, was drawn from the William Shaw Academy in Bowes where 100 boys were encouraged by hunger pang and regular beating to better appreciate the delights of education and manners.

So let that be a lesson to you, my four legged friend, as we head out onto the moor.

Wackford Beard is straying onto very dodgy ground in my humble opinion.

Border terrier. Humble? Never

There are a number of oddities on this walk. The first is a stretch of upland road lined on either side by ominous Ministry of Defence signs warning that we're walking through a poison gas area. Very welcoming. But if poison gas makes it dangerous to stray onto the moorland on either side why is it safe to walk down the road in the middle? I think we'll leave that as a bureaucratic imponderable and, breathing as little as possible, move swiftly on.

And then there's the river that disappears. We've reached God's Bridge, a huge slab of natural rock through which the River Greta sometimes runs in spate. But this afternoon the river's gone away. For much of the year it shyly settles into its limestone foundations and runs underground.

Ahead of us is Hong Kong – a woodland that stands sharp on the skyline and that we can see all the way round this walk. Why it's called Hong Kong even the locals have forgotten. We know it was planted by a worthy called Dugdale who may have made his money in the Hong

Kong trade, but beyond that its international connections are a mystery.

High, wide and handsome views shared with tumbling lapwings and pierced by the occasional plaintive cry of curlew give way to gentler, riverside pastures. A set of treacherous stepping stones which are obviously designed for dogs rather than people ensures that one of us paddles back into Bowes with wet feet.

The town's dominated on this squelching approach by the stark outline of the castle keep. It was built for King Henry II as a sort of sub clause in stone to remind the Scots of the peace treaty they'd just signed. And it worked. Good King Henry could safely ignore Bowes and go adventuring in Ireland and France instead when he wasn't falling out with his disloyal sons and getting into bother with The Pope for the murder of Thomas Becket.

Isn't it amazing what a sweep of history you can cram into just eight miles.

And next time you're asked in the pub quiz or when playing Trivial Pursuit what town links Wackford Squeers, Henry II, Hong Kong and a poison gas field, you'll know. Won't you.

The Approach to Moscow

I was prepared to string along with him when he pretended to go to Hong Kong but this could turn into the cold war.

George W. Bush might be a good name for a belligerent Border Terrier.

---

5 gentle miles, some on by roads, which should take no more than two or three hours.

Route on OS Explorer OL 43 Hadrian's Wall starting and finishing at map reference NY633673.

Gilsland Spa was once the place to be seen. The rich and fashionable would come here to take the waters. Pleasure gardens and tea rooms and even a lantern-lit ballroom were built on the banks of the River Irthing. A landslip eventually did for them but the sulphurous source still runs. Having tasted and, more particularly, smelt the Gilsland waters you'll perhaps wish it didn't.

Wild garlic along the riverbank soon counteracts the stench of rotten eggs as we wander along tree shaded paths to The Popping Stone. One of the famous visitors to Gilsland was Sir Walter Scott who met his French wife here and he came to this boulder by the river to pop the question. It's smaller now because of the romantic little habit of young ladies scraping bits off to hide under their pillows. It's said that the sliver of stone would make them sleep soundly and dream of the man they were going to marry. I suppose it was the Victorian equivalent of a night's clubbing and twelve Bacardi Breezers.

But to make Gilsland chime with modern times they've installed another boulder further along the river called the unpopping stone. Put a bit of that under your pillow and it will tell you when you're going to get divorced. Only joking.

And he calls me cynical.

As we climb along the misty river we begin to hear the roar of Crammel Linn, the swirling pool in the gorge. It's a thirty feet deep cascade of turbulent water stained brown by the peat mosses of Spadeadam Waste. A spectacularly beautiful place just a few yards from the perimeter of what was once one of the most secret defence establishments in the   country.

Spadeadam was the home of Britain's space programme. It was here that they developed and tested the Blue Streak Rocket until Prime Minister Harold Wilson decided that the money would be better spent by allowing British Leyland to build the Austin 1100. Anyone who ever tried to keep the body on an Austin 1100 will know it wasn't his smartest political decision.

More recently Spadeadam has been used as an electronic aiming mark for RAF low flying exercises so you might have the occasional rude awakening as a Tornado or some such just misses your left ear. There's a story, perhaps apocryphal, that during the Cold War a layout of Moscow airport was built at Spadeadam so that pilots would be able to acquaint themselves with their prime target. If the story's not true it's a pity because, on our right is the real Moscow – a farm on the edge of the moor. The day we were there it started to snow. So to avoid Napoleonic humiliation and before Mother Russia takes her revenge we head down to the A69, whistling excerpts from the 1812 Overture as we go.

Let me tell you. Classic FM has nothing to fear.

The Secret Canal

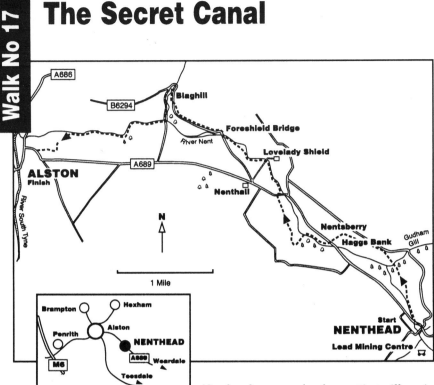

Nenthead may not be the prettiest village in the Pennines but be thankful for small mercies. At least his internationalist phase seems to have worked itself out. Timbuktu on Tyne will have to wait for another day.

8 miles downhill which, with time for exploration, should take about 5 hours including an hour for the underground tour.

Route on OS Explorer OL 31 North Pennines, Teesdale and Weardale starting at map reference NY781436 and finishing at map reference NY719465

Details of the underground tour from the Nenthead Mines Visitor Centre, telephone 01434 382037.

We're standing in a valley that was once home to the biggest lead mining complex in Europe. There are thousands of miles of tunnels and adits honeycombing the hills. A section has been opened to demonstrate the conditions the lead miners of Nenthead had to work in from Elizabethan times to the twentieth century. At first sight they hadn't improved a lot. Dripping, stooped tunnels open into caverns that echo to footfall and whisper and a constant background of running water. Occasionally there are chimneys through the rock lined with wooden ladders that gave access to older, ghostly levels.

But we're going to be following the grandest tunnel of them all. Three hundred feet below where we're standing in the mine yard is the start of an engineering project that was the eighteenth century equivalent of the Channel Tunnel. The Nent Force Level cost millions of pounds and took sixty three years to build. Deep under the bed of the meandering River Nent it runs six miles from Nenthead to Alston. Through a landscape that once thundered with industrial bravado we're walking by roads and tracks that link the tiny communities scattered across the fell breast. Here and there are the barred metal doors of mine levels pouring stained water out of the hill. After a bit of searching we find the top of the shaft at Nentsberry Haggs and look down into the void.

One hundred and fifty feet down the shaft there's the entrance to a horse level that runs the one and a half miles to Nenthead. The waterfall that tumbles out of that shimmers and fractures another two hundred feet into the canal that carried freight traffic three and a quarter miles from here to Alston. If you've remembered to pack a powerful torch in your rucksack you may just be able to see a glimpse of it.

Typical. We're half way through a walk, miles from nowhere and beardbrain reminds us that we should have packed a torch.

It's said that in very cold weather the warmer air from the canal rises and forms a cloud of mist above the Nentsberry shaft.

The canal was designed by John Smeaton, the first man to describe himself as a civil engineer.

Presumably before Smeaton tidied up the profession they'd been uncivil engineers.

He's probably best known as the builder of the Eddystone Lighthouse but this was his most innovative project. It wasn't an unqualified success. The sponsors of the canal had hoped to find new veins of workable lead as they drove through the hill. They didn't. But the underground waterway drained the existing mines where water had always been a problem and allowed another seventy years of mining employment. Riverside paths take us past abandoned sluice gates to the waterfall of Nent Force and a mystery. The Alston end of Britain's most secret canal has been mislaid. I know it's hard to credit that you can mislay a tunnel that was big enough to take ore barges and even pleasure craft, but they have. It probably happened when they cleared spoil heaps on the edge of the town. All we can see of it today is the lintel of a tiny overflow channel in the rocky river bank below Nent Force.

He's probably working up to saying that you should also have packed a bulldozer.

Avoiding Heartbeat

N

1 Mile

Beck Hole
Combs Wood
Incline Cottage
Goathland
Eller Beck
Julian Park
Mallyan Spout
Waterfall
West Beck
Dismantled Railway
North York Moors Railway
Hollin House Farm
Nelly Eyre Foss
Waterfall
Hazel Head Farm
Hunt House Road
Wheeldale Gill
Start & Finish
P
Roman Road
Wheeldale Lodge
Youth Hostel
Stepping Stones

Middlesbrough
Darlington
Whitby
GOATHLAND
A171
A1
A169
A170
Scarborough
Pickering
A64
Malton
York

After all the years we've been trundling round the north of England he really ought to know that Goathland is not the place for a peaceful walk full, as it is, of gawping trippers and dogs with no breeding.

If any of you bought this book at the gift shop in Goathland while waiting to visit the garage that featured in the television programme 'Heartbeat' it's sorry from me and a grudging apology from him.

6 miles of reasonably easy going which will take no more than 3 hours.

Route on OS Explorer OL 27 North York Moors Eastern Area starting and finishing at NZ814989.

Just to prove a terrier wrong we're going to stroll out of Goathland, find solitude and great walking and make no reference apart from this one to a certain television programme which is apparently filmed in these parts. In fact I wonder why these coachloads of people are wandering aimlessly down the village street.

Just half a mile from the crush we're in a secret valley at the foot of the tallest waterfall in the North York Moors – Mallyan Spout. It seems to be pouring in slow motion down a picturesque wall of creviced rock. Its spray drips from ledges layered with moss and fern and highlights the piercingly green young foliage of the beech trees that crowd around it.

I think I can feel a sylvan glade coming on.

No, it's Beck Hole, huge stepping stones across the river where, it's said, a fearsome dragon used to live.

The sylvan glade might be preferable.

This dragon dined exclusively on local virgins and, according to legend, was eventually slain by a great warrior with mystical powers.

More likely he starved to death.

We wander past the farm at Julian Park, the setting for our second slab of local folklore. This was the lair of the Gytrash which, despite the way it sounds, wasn't a character from a programme on Channel 5. The owner of Julian Park wanted to build a new castle and the tradition at the time was that, to bring good luck to the building, it needed a human sacrifice. The prettiest local virgin was brought from the village and walled up in the foundations where she popped her clogs.

(By the way, if you're presently thinking of building a new house I should point out that there are now EU rules which forbid that sort of thing.)

Anyhow, the spirit of the dead virgin rose from the grave and bumped off the owner of Julian Park who, in turn, became the ravening Gytrash. Part vampire, part goat it terrorised the area and devoured every virgin it could get its cloven hooves on.

Which, of course, is why the aforementioned dragon starved to death.

He does so love being able to tie up the loose ends.

We climb out into the clear air of Wheeldale Moor to look for one of the most fascinating archaeological remains in the district – Wade's Causeway. You have to cut through the miasma of folklore here as well. It was supposedly built by a giant called Wade for his wife Bel to make it easier for her to drive her pigs across the moor. Now Dragons and Guytrashes are OK but a pig keeping Giantess called Bel stretches credibility too far.

At first sight it's a Roman road. Except the Romans didn't build roads to this design. It may be a rare piece of evidence that supposedly backward Britons had already mastered the skills of highway construction long before the Empire arrived with its fancy new ways.

On the other hand it could be the giant's pig road.

Which would explain present company. I think I'll hitch a lift with a passing tripper back to Goathland.

A Stroll to Crackpot Hall

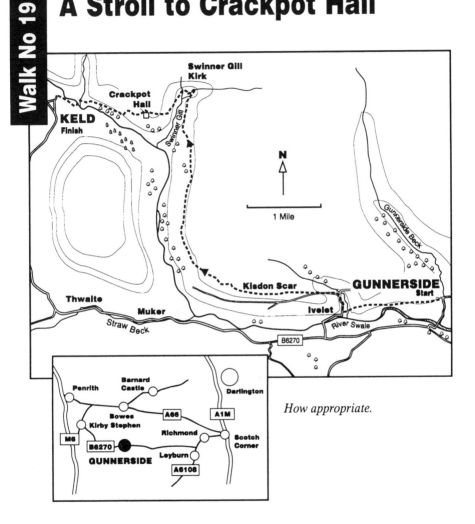

How appropriate.

A strenuous 5 mile walk that should keep you out of mischief for about 4 hours.

Route on OS Explorer OL 30 Yorkshire Dales Northern and Central starting at map reference SD951982 and finishing at map reference NY892011

We're climbing out of Swaledale into Swinnergill, constantly stopping to look back through the drizzle into a smudged watercolour of the valley floor with its softened patchwork of fields and farms. Our track takes us along a ledge in the escarpment heading for a jumble of broken buildings at the mouth of the branch valley of East Grain. We're back in lead country. The ruins were once the Swinnergill smelt mill and we find what shelter we can by the cold, empty fireplace of what must have been the mill office.

One good thing about a drizzle day is that you've more chance of peace and quiet. Part of this route coincides with Wainwright's Coast to Coast walk and in good weather on bank holiday weekends it can be a bit of a procession. Nobody else is daft enough to be processing today.

A chunter of agreement is heard from where a length of baler string emerges from behind a rock.

There wouldn't have been much peace and quiet here two hundred and fifty years ago. This was a battlefield in which the footsoldiers were miners from rival prospecting companies. They sabotaged each others' workings. They diverted steams to flood neighbouring levels and even threw a miner or two to their deaths down a shaft or hush gutter.

Good old fashioned Yorkshire Dales hospitality. That's what I say.

A detour that involves a paddle up the rocky beck bottom of the Swinnergill gorge takes us back to troubled times a hundred years earlier. Partly hidden by a waterfall and under a natural arch of rock is The Kirk. It's a low ceilinged cave that was used as a secret church. At times of religious intolerance dissenters from the Dales communities would make their way up here, at times having to wade knee deep through a swollen beck to gather together and celebrate their illicit religion.

As we walk up the path out of Swinnergill we enter a landscape of ruins from a time when the population of these dales was ten, maybe twenty times what it is today. Abandoned cottages and broken barns and farm houses are the gravestones marking the passing of these little communities. The grandest ruin of the lot....

Old greybeard is chancing his arm making remarks like that.

The grandest ruin of the lot is Crackpot Hall with its spectacular views along the river to Muker. It was still a working farm in the 1950s but then the mining subsidence took one nibble too many out of its foundations and it fell down. The kitchen wall has disappeared but the range is still standing. There's a tin bath in front of the fire and there are shreds of patterned paper on the walls of bedrooms with no floors.

It's an eerie place where you can almost hear the shouts of children playing and the sounds of a bustling farm yard. But maybe it's just the quickening wind busying itself with the long slow job of natural demolition.

Raq and Ruin head for home.

The Gunmaker of Cragside

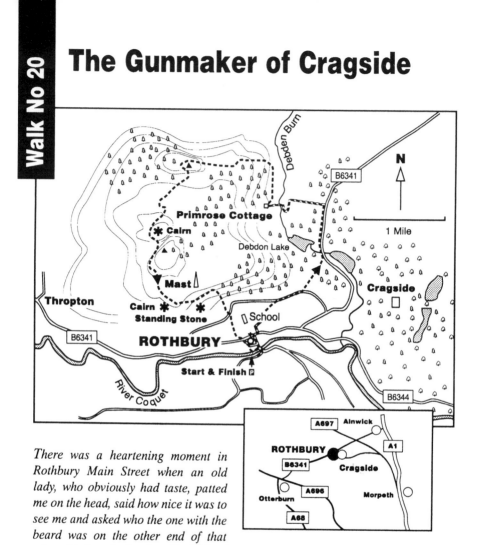

There was a heartening moment in Rothbury Main Street when an old lady, who obviously had taste, patted me on the head, said how nice it was to see me and asked who the one with the beard was on the other end of that miserable length of string. He did his best to smile but you could tell it got to him.

---

5 strolling miles which will take no more than a couple of hours plus however long you want to spend exploring the gardens at Cragside.

Route on OS Explorer 332 Alnwick and Amble starting and finishing in Rothbury at map reference NU057015

Today Rothbury looks as if its greatest excitement would be the monthly meeting of the Mothers' Union.

But in the sixteenth century it had the reputation of being a sort of border Dodge City, renowned the length and breadth of Britain for its drinking, gambling and brawling. Rothbury's High Noon came with the arrival of Bernard Gilpin, a Vicar from Houghton Le Spring. Playing the Gary Cooper part he set about the troublesome locals, banged a few heads together (in a Christian sort of way, of course) and generally cleaned the place up. Once the bodies had been removed from Main Street they gave him the honorary title of The Apostle of the North. It has a much nicer ring to it than Sheriff, don't you think?

Anyhow, we're heading out from Boot Hill through lanes tumbling with foxgloves to explore the big country. We're in search not of gunslingers but of the great gunmaker. This was a landscape that touched the iron soul of Lord Armstrong who escaped here from the pandaemonium of his Tyneside armaments factories.

From the hill above Rothbury we can look down into the paradise valley that he and Lady Armstrong created at Cragside. Having built a modest holiday cottage big enough to re-house half of Gateshead they set about reshaping the hillsides around it. No garden designer was allowed to meddle with the great works. It was the power of their own imagination that planned the woodlands and rock gardens and water courses of Cragside. Admittedly they had one hundred and fifty gardeners to do the dirty finger nail bits but, even so, the Armstrongs' choice of plants and eye for shape and detail created one of the great gardens of England. Today just ten National Trust gardeners try to keep the spirit of the Armstrong dream alive.

We climb out from Cragside to heathered hill tops with wide views over gently rolling Northumbrian landscapes. Cragside itself was merely the hub of a grand wheel of countryside. Across the hills Lord Armstrong laid out miles of carriageways where his guests and visiting business associates could take the air and know that their host owned virtually all that they surveyed.

So peaceful is the setting that it's hard to square with the source of the brass that paid for it. Armstrong's innovative guns doubled and trebled the world's killing capacity. But the Great Gunmaker considered himself enlightened and even handed. His proud boast was that in many conflicts in distant lands he supplied guns to both sides. So that's all right then.

Through rocky outcrops and over a springing carpet of heather we walk back across the hill to Rothbury where a lady, obviously heading for the Mothers' Union meeting, recognises Raq and makes a great fuss of him and tells me off for dragging the poor thing about on a scruffy bit of string.

He'll be wanting a star on the kennel door next.

I told you he wasn't best pleased.

Snow on the Wastwater
Screes Boulder Field
Photo: Bill Guest

Sunset at Wastwater
Photo: Bill Guest

Raq on Castle Crag
Borrowdale
Photo: Eric Robson

Raq and Ruin on Latrigg
Photo: © Granada

Burial Cairn on Bewick Hill
Photo: © Granada

Gatehouse at Whalley Abbey
Photo: © Granada

Brimham Rocks
Photo: © Granada

Northumbrian Landscape
Photo: © Granada

ii

The Ravenglass and Eskdale
Railway
Photo: Bill Guest

Ravenglass Estuary
Photo: Bill Guest

Ashgill Force
Photo: © Granada

The Pennines above Garrigill
Photo: © Granada

Teesside from Eston Nab
Photo: © Granada

Sunset from Stainmore
Photo: Eric Robson

Fountains Abbey
Photo: © Granada

Heading for the Hills
Photo: © Granada

Cynophobia in Kendal

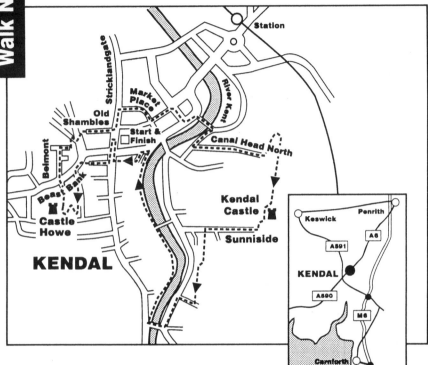

If you're challenged in the leg department, with two rather than the regulation four, you perhaps won't recognise the word. He's obviously trying for the sympathy vote suggesting he's got a phobia about dogs, poor dear. But two can play at that game. Let me suggest an alternative title.

Pogonophobia in Kendal

Even with two legs I bet you can guess that's something to do with a phobia about beards.

---

2 miles that you could do on your hands and knees in a couple of hours.

Route on the Kendal Town Mini Guide available from the Tourist Information Office. Start and finish at Kendal Town Hall in Highgate.

The last word on this walk can be found in the Oxford English Dictionary.

This is Out of Town in town. A walk to keep up your sleeve to use on one of those days when the weather's so bloody awful that you're even tempted to watch daytime telly.

But no. Resist the blandishments of Richard Whiteley. (Blandishment – the art of telling bad jokes to a woman who can add up in her head) Switch off City Hospital. (Hospital –a place where patients were once treated but which has now been turned into a television studio or a unit for giving medical attention to pets) Turn your back on The Weakest Link. (Weakest Link – a fault in the DNA sequencing of some individuals which leaves them with a predisposition to devise, produce or present truly appalling television programmes)

Even at the full extent of my string I think I'm beginning to suffer from Glossophobia. (Glossophobia – an exaggerated fear of talking, particularly when the talk is being strained through a beard and moustache). I made that last bit up.

There's long been a tradition of endurance walking in Kendal. The Stricklandgate Stroll involved walking up one side of the street and crawling back down the other having had a half pint in every one of the fifty or so pubs that you stumble into on the way. Nowadays they have signs on the lamp posts warning that you'll be fined if you're caught drinking. And we call it progress.

But he digresses. (Digression – an ill judged attempt at humour when one ought to be getting on with the walk)

We're heading away from the rumble of the Highgate traffic and within thirty seconds are in the eighteenth century. Kendal, the old grey town, is a maze of yards and alleyways linked by steep flights of stone steps. Crowding over them the houses and workshops of a disappeared trade. It was in these cramped, insanitary lanes that generations of weavers produced Kendal Green, the coarse woollen cloth that was worn by the English bowmen at Agincourt.

Round the next corner there's a reminder that Kendal people were very fond of the marauding Scots. So keen, in fact that they gave them their very own burial ground.

Out of an alleyway into Branthwaite Brow to marvel at the cast iron houses of Kendal. When the street was widened in 1851 the designers of the scheme created more space by taking down the fronts of the houses and replacing them with a riveted sheet of cast iron. It might have caught on as a building technique but for the Titanic.

On our way out of town we come across a little factory yard that's known as the Kendal Brown House. Here, for hundreds of years they've been making another of Kendal's most famous exports. In giant metal pestles with huge oak mortars they grind tobacco. And then they do what with it? They powder it and then stuff it up their noses? Yes, it's snuff and Kendal snuff has even tickled the adenoids of the rich and famous. Napoleon sniffed seven pounds of it a month –what else was there to do on St. Helena? George III's consort Charlotte liked it so much that she was known as Snuffy Charlotte.

I'm sure he's making some of this up.

Under shallow arched bridges and through redundant locks we're walking the northern reach of a canal that once linked Kendal to Lancaster. It was known as The Black and White – coal in and limestone out. Enjoy this bit while you can because they're thinking of opening it again as a working waterway.

And then, to round off our walk, we're climbing out to a vantage point over the town by Kendal's new castle. New in this context means that it was built by Norman barons in the middle of the thirteenth century to secure the turbulent north west frontier. The old castle presumably had links with Methuselah.

He should know.

There are times, I mused as we wandered back to Highgate, when an uncivil travelling companion can bring on an attack of bathmophobia.

Upper Coquetdale

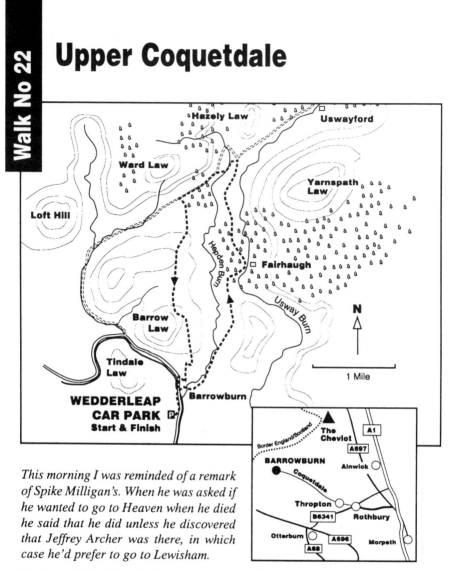

This morning I was reminded of a remark of Spike Milligan's. When he was asked if he wanted to go to Heaven when he died he said that he did unless he discovered that Jeffrey Archer was there, in which case he'd prefer to go to Lewisham.

The bearded bathmaphobe is planning a walk in the Arcadian hills of Upper Coquetdale. I think I'd prefer to go to Lewisham.

---

5 miles with a fair bit of ascent which will take about 4 hours.

Route on OS Outdoor Leisure 16 The Cheviot Hills starting and finishing at map reference NT866103

The hills seem to stretch forever, rolling away in gentle, undulating swathes of green silk into the high Cheviots.

On our climb out from the valley we pass what must have been one of the most remote and privileged schools in the north of England. Privileged by its spectacular setting but also because of a remarkable man who was its headmaster. Andrew Blythe was a one armed, self taught gypsy from the nearby township of Kirk Yethom which was the court of the border gypsy kings. By all accounts Blythe was revered by the children he taught. His simple lessons brought the mysteries and delights of the world alive in this lonely place. He was also a distant relative of a man who would, one day, become President of the United States of America. William Jefferson Clinton was a Blythe by birth. Andrew Blythe would have approved of Bill Clinton's vision of international affairs. What the Godfearing headmaster from Coquetdale would have made of his grasp of domestic affairs we can only surmise.

A long and winding track takes us across a low watershed into one of the many secret valleys that hide in the skirts of The Cheviot. This is a landscape emptied by the Border Diaspora – the equivalent of the Highland Clearances. Hundreds of families, like Bill Clinton's ancestors, were driven from here by poverty and the depredations of greedy landlords to find a better life in American and Australia.

At Fairhaugh there's an old shepherd's cottage boarded up now but, blind and frail as it is, still standing as a reminder of the enduring agricultural community that flourished here from the days in the thirteenth century when the Cistercian monks of Newminster grazed their flocks on these hills until the 1960s when trees ousted the last of the shepherds.

We climb on towards the highest remaining farm in the Cheviots at Uswayford – Uzzyford if you have to ask directions to it locally. Kids from here would have to walk down to the school, snow permitting, and they reckoned those trudges morning and night would add up to twelve and a half thousand miles by the time they heard the last schoolyard bell. Now that thought puts a spring in our step as we head back into the valley past a dilapidated building stuck in the middle of nowhere that was once the Locarno of the Cheviots.

Apparently they were great dancers, the border shepherds and their ladies. The highlight of the social season was the beaters' ball which was a dance not a complaint occasioned by the wearing of overly tight plus fours. But one tragic night the dancers went at it a bit too energetically and some of them fell through the floor of the old community hall. The man who had the shooting rights on the estate built them this new one which was reputed to have the best sprung floor in Northumberland. Today the music is no more. It's now a hay barn with the best sprung floor in Northumberland.

Before he starts whistling selections from Jimmy Shand I think it's time for a quickstep home. Lewisham anyone?

The Metro Centre Walk

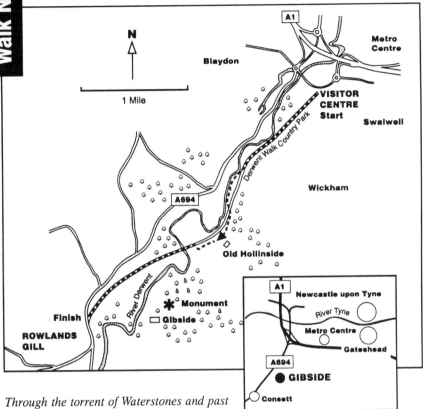

Through the torrent of Waterstones and past the fearsome Gap. Next to Timberland. Boots to Greenwoods. Monsoon to River Island. Oasis to Littlewoods......

Top Man's lost it.

---

3 very gentle miles which will take just a couple of hours.

Route on OS Explorer 316 Newcastle Upon Tyne, OS Explorer 308 Durham and Sunderland and OS Explorer 307 Consett and Derwent Reservoir. Starts at map reference NZ200621 and finishes at NZ167585

This is a therapeutic walk for shopping addicts. It weans you away from the Metro Centre car park into the age of enlightenment. We'll even give you a 10p off your next purchase voucher if you do it.

Just half a mile from the car park the chatter of the checkouts has faded and you're probably having a panic attack. But just take a deep breath and enjoy what, in the eighteenth century, they would have called a sylvan glade. A tunnel of sunlit woodland takes us across the site of what was once the biggest iron works in Europe.

We're walking out into the Derwent valley which has been treasured as a wildlife corridor into the heart of industrial Tyneside for 150 years. Further along the valley we'll come to something called the Butterfly Bridge where Victorian gentlemen cavorting with butterfly nets would come to gather specimens for their collections. Don't try that sort of stunt today or you'll end up in the environmental terrorists' equivalent of Camp X Ray.

This used to be the line of the Derwent Valley Railway that hauled tens of thousands of tons of coal and iron ore to a squalor of local industries and the staithes on the Tyne. But the retreat of heavy industry from the banks of the Derwent was so sudden and so dramatic it's as if the centuries of manufacture had never been. Nature has taken its territory back. There are even otters in the river now as there would have been in Saxon times when the ancient and disappeared village of Winlaton huddled round a ford in the river. By it ran Clockburn Lonnen, one of those almost forgotten highways. It's just a narrow, muddy track now but for centuries it was the most important route from Durham to the north. On the fifteenth of July 1650 Oliver Cromwell passed this way at the head of sixteen thousand men on their way to fight the Battle of Dunbar.

We climb out to a grand viewpoint by the ruins of the thirteenth century fortified manor of Hollinside. Judging by the contents of its rubbish tip there was nothing they liked better in the thirteenth century than sitting round the great log fire swilling a few cans of lager and washing down their cheeseburgers with the odd bottle of cheap sherry. But, then, the Hardings of Hollinside were big men with big appetites. The place was always known as The Giant's Castle which of course we have to dismiss as the superstitions of simple country folk, except that when they opened the Harding family vault in Whickham Cemetery they found the skeletons of men more than seven feet tall.

But if the Hardings had stayed out of the clutches of the cemetery long enough (five centuries long enough) they'd have met their match in Lord Strathmore. It was claret, learning and polite society that fuelled his imagination. He imagined the arrival of a monstrous machine that would encroach on his aristocratic slumbers and probably keep the servants awake. He imagined the end of the world as he knew it with common people under his bedroom window, smelly, coarse and, most probably, revolutionary. The only way of keeping the terrible threat at bay was to insist that the Devil's railway was diverted across an expensive viaduct outside his estate. Only if that happened could he fully devote his energies to celebrating the ascent of man and its greatest manifestation – British Liberty. In the long run both the railway and Lord Strathmore's vision lost. The railway's shut and very common people like us can walk along it and majestic Gibside, his haven in a world hurtling to madness, is a sad ruin across the valley. But towering above Lord Strathmore's redundant pleasure grounds the statue of British Liberty still dominates our view from the viaduct and the Derwent Valley landscape.

It's interesting to imagine how the coal miners and iron workers of the Derwent Valley would have reacted to having a sculptor amongst them. Limp wristed profession sculpting; not a patch on carving coal out of an eighteen inch seam.

But I'm sure they changed their minds when they saw Mr Christopher Richardson, sculptor, on his way to work. He had to climb into a basket with his two assistants and then was hauled by block and tackle to the top of a one hundred and forty feet high stone pillar where the builders had left a plain block of stone covered with a wooden

The CKP

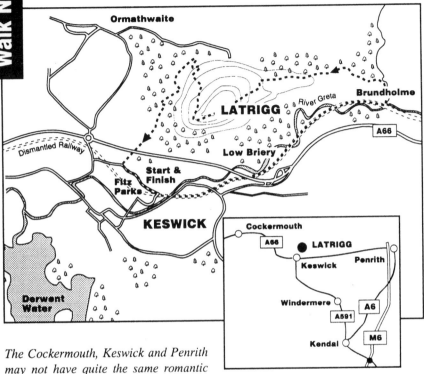

The Cockermouth, Keswick and Penrith may not have quite the same romantic ring to it as the Atchison, Topeka and Santa Fe but it was one of the most scenic railways in Britain until the soulless accountants got to it.

Any soulless accountant who's bought the book should take the connecting service to walk twenty five which is standing at platform four.

---

5 and a bit miles with a stiff climb out onto Latrigg. 3 hours.

Route on OS Explorer OL 4 The English Lakes North West starting and finishing at map reference NY272238

Details of plans to reopen the CKP from www.ckp-railways.co.uk

---

We're standing under the glass canopy at Keswick station which is now a car park but where on the 2nd of January 1865 flags were fluttering, the band was playing and the first passenger service on the CKP was about depart.

There's a danger, a very real danger of the bearded fat controller doing the sound effects if I don't haul on this conveniently placed length of string and drag him away down the line.

Just outside Keswick we come to what was once the workers' halt at Low Briery. It was a bustling industrial complex. A water powered bobbin mill used to turn out 40 million bobbins a year to be exported as far afield as Uruguay and Hong Kong. Here they manufactured the bobbins that were used in the making of Queen Elizabeth II's Coronation gown. There was a pencil mill and a textile plant known locally as The Fancy Bottoms Mill. Fortunately the fancy bottoms in question were trimmings for waistcoats.

Through abandoned cuttings lined with thickets of birch we walk over half moon bowstring bridges into the Greta Gorge. Even though it only runs for seven or eight miles the Greta can be a spectacular river in heavy weather, but then it does have the wastes of Blencathra as a header tank.

Another bridge, this time apparently upside down with the half moon lattice of ironwork dipping towards the river. And a word of warning. This line was designed by the engineer Thomas Bouch who was best known as the designer of the ill fated Tay Bridge which fell down taking a trainload of passengers with it. We hurry on and start the long climb out onto Latrigg with emerging views to the south and west.

When the greatest fellwalking writer of them all, Alfred Wainwright, came up here in 1960 he looked out at the panorama of Lakeland summits and wondered if there would be mountains like this in Heaven. In fact he wondered if he'd strayed into Heaven already.

If any soulless accountant happened to miss the connecting service at

Keswick and tagged along with us I bet even he would be forced to glance up from the profit and loss ledger and marvel at the mountains crowding around us. Brooding over our shoulder is Skiddaw. Away to the East on our left are the outlyers of Lakeland, Great and Little Mell Fell dominated by Clough Head. There's the run of The Dodds out to Helvellyn and ahead of us, across the Greta Valley, Bleaberry Fell. Over its shoulder and more than twelve miles away there are Crinkle Crags and further right again the Scafell Range. Below us an extraordinarily blue Derwentwater with Castle Crag locked in the Jaws of Borrowdale and Catbells rising through a sunny morning to Dale Head. Beyond that Hindscarth and then Robinson that looks as if a giant has taken a mouthful out of the side of the mountain. On the far horizon High Stile and Red Pike whilst closer there's the long ridge out to the bulk of Grasmoor before the proud, almost Alpine summit of Grisedale Pike drops away into the Whinlatter Pass.

Dog stifles yawn and looks longingly at a flock of sheep grazing amongst the shadows of the Castlerigg Stone Circle on a hill across the valley.

But look on the bright side. As we plunge off Latrigg back to Keswick at least the views have taken beardorama's mind off the steam trains. Or have I barked too soon?

"It must have been a great sight with one of those reliable, resilient 0-6-0's making smoke while hauling a heavy train through the Greta Gorge. They used to call them Cauliflowers, and do you know why?"

He's going to tell me, whatever I say.

"They were called cauliflowers because the symbol of the London and North Western Railway that owned them looked like....."

Don't tell me – a cauliflower.

Sad. Very sad.

Holy Island

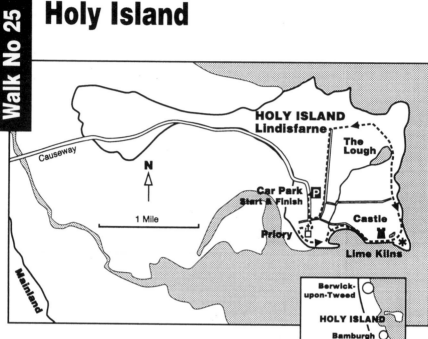

This morning Michael Fish said the weather would be reasonably settled with the chance of a few scattered showers. I think he should abandon the state of the art Meteorological Office satellite imaging computer and hang up a piece of damp seaweed instead. He might have more chance of getting it right. When we arrived at Holy Island it was blowing a hooley with occasional splats of horizontal sleet. Boats were straining at their moorings and we were straining to stand up.

Thank you, Michael Fish. I must invite you to join us on a walk some day. When the weather's settled of course.

---

4 easy miles which should take a couple of hours.

Route on OS Explorer 340 Holy Island and Bamburgh starting and finishing at map reference NU126424

Access to Holy Island is across a tidal causeway. Details of the tides from the tourist office in Berwick-upon-Tweed or www.lindisfarne.org.uk

The sea rages in across the causeway and the dog looks like a bouffant border terrier....

Steady.

... and we plunge into the walk between a strange collection of blackened, upturned boats that have escaped the breaker's yard to end their days as fishermen's sheds. A flying lobster pot decides to come with us.

We're on the shore where St Aidan baptised the Northumbrians in the seventh century; where he created the spiritual heart of the golden age of enlightenment that would turn this corner of northern England into the cultural centre of Europe. For a while. The fabric of the priory that marks his passing was eventually destroyed by pagan Viking invaders. What they couldn't destroy was the spirit of peace in a chaotic world that still haunts the ruins of Holy Island's lonely priory.

A tanker wallows in a mountainous sea as we walk out past the castle on its towering plug of rock. It's where Gormenghast meets Disneyland. A confection in stone designed by the celebrated architect Sir Edwin Lutyens for a former editor of Country Life Magazine.

While I was marvelling at the rampant ego that could conceive of such a pretence Raq discovered the shelter of a hole in the ground. Dripping subterranean tunnels and vaults that are all that remain of Holy Island's industrial revolution. They're the remains of kilns built to produce agricultural lime that was sent from here to the north of Scotland in a fleet of five ships that plied between Holy Island and Dundee. Pity the men who sailed them in weather like this. They must have been using digestive tracts that, like Iron Bru, were made from girders.

Along a sweeping strand of rounded and sea worn stones we head for the north coast. To the place where the coach parties that mob Holy Island's car parks never go. Grey sky blends with greyer sea, the join blurred by wind whipped spray. This is elemental Holy Island where Aidan and Cuthbert found the voice of God in nature. On rock strata exposed by the pounding of heavy seas down the ages there are the fossilised remains of trees trapped in compressed sediments since the dawn of time. We turned our faces to the weather and waited for the sunset. When it came it was breathtaking – Turner and John Piper squabbling over the best use of the canvas.

If you don't find it a mysterious and magical place your soul needs a service.

Border terriers are God's creatures, too. And this one's wet, cold and bored. Thank you Mr. Fish. Thank you.

To the Sour Milk Hills

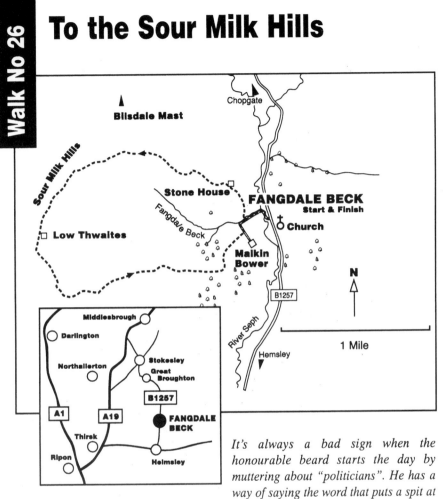

It's always a bad sign when the honourable beard starts the day by muttering about "politicians". He has a way of saying the word that puts a spit at either end and a grunt in the middle. And for some reason politicos had got an inch and a half above his moustache as we set out this morning from Fangdale Beck onto the moor.

5 strenuous miles which will take around three hours. Note for dogs (and for that matter people) with short, fat, hairy legs there's some walking through deep heather on the moorland section.

Route on OS Explorer OL 26 North York Moors Western Area starting and finishing at map reference SE573946.

77

Not just politicians, my hairy friend. Overpaid Government consultants, corporate time servers who think a shower of e.mails is a day's work and public relations advisors and counsellors who have a mission to convince us that whatever happens is somebody else's fault all fit the bill just as well.

Keep the head down, the nose in the heather and don't wag your tail is my advice.

Take the phone box in Fangdale Beck. Or to be more precise take the attitude of the bureaucrats of BT to the phone box in Fangdale Beck.

BT (Once British telecom but by the time you read this probably Conphonia or some such gibberish name) tried to take the village's perfectly serviceable Edwardian phone box and replace it with one of those draughts round the ankles modern jobs. Leaving aside the fact that the new box was obviously designed by someone who needed a trained Labrador and a white stick the residents of Fangdale Beck just wanted to keep the old box which was entirely adequate and kinder on the ankles. They rebelled, BT retreated, and the old box is still there – or at least it was when we visited. Make a call from it as you pass by whether you need to or not.

From the village huddled round a gentle stream we climb steadily to the moorland top. In the distance over our left shoulder is the Bilsdale television mast which you might be tempted to describe as a scar on an otherwise perfect landscape – except that on this occasion we're in a book that's associated with a television programme which was transmitted by the Bilsdale mast so we'd better restrain ourselves.

There's a long, slow walk through deep heather which has Raq alternately bounding and disappearing in a most appealing sort of way.

His "appealing" is my heather rash.

All around us are the melancholy remains of abandoned farmsteads; victims of agricultural policies that are steadily driving people out of the uplands. Around each farm house there's a patch of vivid green where centuries of hard labour won the land from the moor. But of course that dedicated work matters not a jot to political policy makers and Treasury Mandarins whose experience of patches of vivid green is limited to the park in Islington or the surrounds of a villa in Tuscany. They're quite capable of deciding that farming is an expensive and outmoded luxury for a dynamic, advanced country like Britain. Much more sensible to create a new government agency called OffLand or some such which will care for the countryside at even greater public expense.

But what the quangoids would never know, and what the outmoded farmers learned from long experience is that this tract of moorland has a particular mix of flora that had a strange effect on dairy cattle – hence its name The Sour Milk Hills.

And then it's downhill all the way for us as well as for the farming that's hanging on by the merest fingernail in these high, wild places. Down to what was one of the oldest pubs in Yorkshire. The thatched Sun Inn at Bilsdale was first licenced in 1714 when beer was one and threepence a gallon. It was delivered by horse drawn dray from Tadcaster by way of Sutton Bank. It's said that if the Sun put in a particularly big order the weight was too much for the dray horses and the barrels had to be offloaded and rolled up the bank by hand.

But when they eventually arrived at the Sun there would have been plenty of willing hands ready to raise a glass and empty them. Visiting gentry, here for the shooting, rubbing shoulders with farmers and jet miners and cloggers. The clogging gangs used to cut Bilsdale alder which was exported to Lancashire to make mill workers' clogs. It was thirsty work. The Bilsdale Brass Band might have been playing in the courtyard. Perhaps there was a cricket match in full swing on the pitch behind the pub. Once the West Indies played here. And in the bar maybe the local bobby, who was an extremely thin man, was winning his bet by folding himself away into the stone bread oven by the fire.

Happy days and not a politician in sight.

The Secret Garden of Rivington Pike

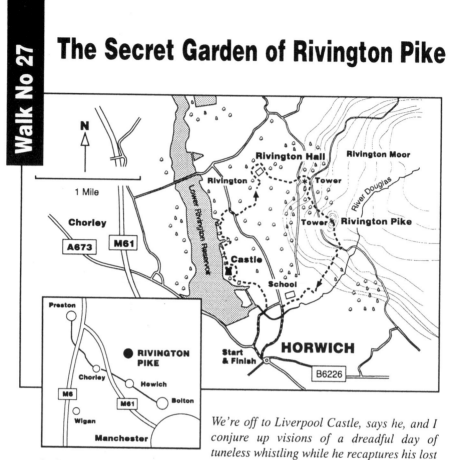

We're off to Liverpool Castle, says he, and I conjure up visions of a dreadful day of tuneless whistling while he recaptures his lost youth. Sergeant Pepper, Yellow submarine, Lucy in the Sky with Diamonds. They'd all sound horribly the same and could be Mantovani's greatest hits if you didn't happen to know that John, Paul, George and Beardo were on tour. In his dreams.

So imagine the relief when we go nowhere near Liverpool but, instead, turn off the motorway into Horwich.

---

5 miles with a long, steady climb out to Rivington Pike summit which will probably take about 3 hours, depending on how much time you spend exploring the secret gardens. Add another hour if you want to push on as far as the quieter summit of Smithills Moor.

Route on OS Explorer 287 West Pennine Moors starting and finishing at map reference SD634119

Horwich was a loco town. It's where the Lancashire and Yorkshire Railway Company built its steam engines. Smoke, noise, grime and pinched rows of back to back houses. An odd place for one of the north of England's richest businessmen to build his holiday cottage. But Lord Leverhulme, manufacturer of Sunlight Soap and founder of the company that became Unilever, did just that.

He liked Horwich. He pampered the town by giving it one of the biggest municipal parks in Britain. He spent money like soapy water. Shortly before the First World War, in a corner of the park, he built a replica of Liverpool Castle. (The real one had been pulled down in the eighteenth century to make way for industrial development.) I imagine that ever since 1912 the Town councillors of Horwich have cursed him for his generosity and his folly. For the children of Horwich the ruins are a dream playground. Dozens of them were running about on the high, frayed battlements the day we were there. For local authority solicitors they're presumably a nightmare of impending litigation.

Rows of little Gareths and Kylies queued up to be on the telly. As we walked away one of them shouted after us that he'd just remembered he couldn't be in the film because his mother didn't know he smoked.

We climb out onto the slopes of Rivington Pike, the hill overlooking Horwich that Lord Leverhulme bought as his own playground. Here he built what was known as The Bungalow. The first version was a prefabricated wooden house that was burned down by a suffragette from Preston. Leverhulme got the message. He built the replacement in stone complete with Winter Gardens and Ballroom. Around it he laid out acres of terraced gardens. There was a lake with sluices that could be opened to give a thirty minute display of aquatechnics through a specially constructed series of waterfalls. There was a Japanese garden with tea houses and lantern - lit islands.

The bungalow's been bulldozed and the gardens are in ruins. Rivington Pike was sold to Liverpool Corporation as the water catchment area for their reservoir in the valley and they refused to allow the bungalow to be turned into a hotel.

We spent an hour wandering through overgrown paths and stairways, past pergolas and decaying summerhouses with their high, hazy views through the encroaching rhododendron over industrial Lancashire. All that remains of the bungalow itself is an area of black and white tiled floor in the grass which used to be the ballroom toilets.

At the top of the garden one building does survive. The three storey pigeon tower with blind, boarded windows stands like an incongruous fragment of a Bavarian castle; a slender counterpoint to the squat beacon tower on the summit that's been our aiming mark on the climb out from the valley.

This isn't a walk that you'll have to yourselves. The hot dog vans on the approach to the summit should give a clue about how well used it is. But you can escape from the crowds by walking just a bit further. From the summit of Rivington Pike you can look out to Winter Hill and Smithills Moor and the expanses of the West Pennine Moors. Ten minutes will take you into peace and a lonely landscape where you can whistle excerpts from the Beatles Greatest Hits without fear of anyone raising as much as a snigger.

Except, of course, the dog.

Byland Abbey and Mount Snever

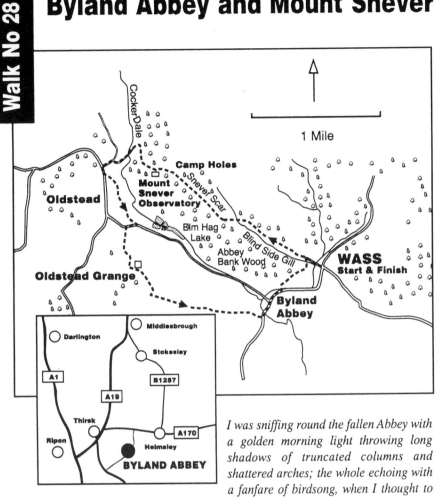

I was sniffing round the fallen Abbey with a golden morning light throwing long shadows of truncated columns and shattered arches; the whole echoing with a fanfare of birdsong, when I thought to myself – if these ruins could talk just imagine how boring they'd be.

A gentle circular walk of just over 4 miles which will take no more than a couple of hours.

Route on OS Explorer 26 North York Moors Western Area starting and finishing at map reference SE555793

It was an enchanted morning and a perfect light. Raq scampering round the Abbey ruins and obviously having a thoroughly good time. And me leaning on a truncated column and imagining what this building, once bigger than Westminster Abbey, would have looked like in all its glory in this Yorkshire setting.

And what an odd reason for putting it here. In the twelfth century the Cistercians built Byland on this site because it was just far enough away from Rievaulx Abbey so they couldn't hear their bells.

We stroll out along dappled woodland tracks climbing steadily towards Mount Snever. There's a bit of crashing through thick undergrowth and clambering through briar patches before we find the mysterious Camp Holes hidden in the wood. A series of deep, meandering trenches are cut into the woodland floor, some 800 yards long. But why? Are we standing in the remains of an Iron Age fort? Could they be, as some suggest, the last redoubt of Edward II's broken army following its defeat by the forces of Robert the Bruce at the Battle of Byland in 1322? More prosaic is the suggestion that they're just quarry trenches from which limestone was extracted to produce the lime mortar used in the construction of Byland Abbey. As nobody really knows, choose which version appeals most to your imagination.

But leave enough space on your imagination's hard drive to allow you to be transported to Victorian times. On the summit of Mount Snever is a folly, built by the businessman John Wormald in the first year of Queen Victoria's reign. It was supposedly built as an observatory but mainly it was a piece of consummate creeping. Its worn plaque proclaims

> *Here hills and waving groves a scene display*
> *And part admit and part exclude the day.*
> *See rich industry smiling on the plains*
> *And peace and plenty tell – Victoria Reigns.*

But did Mr Wormald's investment get him a gong? I suppose the very fact that we're still talking about him all these years on makes it money well spent.

Through the trees ringing the summit there are views of a giant creature striding across the distant hills. It's the white horse of Kilburn - the biggest in England - carved into the limestone slopes by a local headmaster and his pupils. It's just the sort of project that would go down a storm with the organisers of today's National Curriculum - PE, history, mathematics and, if you sang while you dug, music all in the same lesson. Such an efficient use of teaching manpower which would give him time to fill in forms DFE363/1, DFE363/1(amended) and his P45 all on the same afternoon.

Over the years it's been a struggle to prevent the white horse ending up in the knacker's yard. It got a nasty attack of rose bay willow herb. Local farmers struggled to maintain it by dumping huge quantities of fresh limestone. That slipped and the horse now looks as if it's got a hernia. But even put out to grass the white horse of Kilburn is still better known than Mr Wormald which should be a lesson to forelock tuggers everywhere.

On the way back through the fields to Byland I thought to myself – if that horse could speak it would be a bloody miracle.

Tatton Park

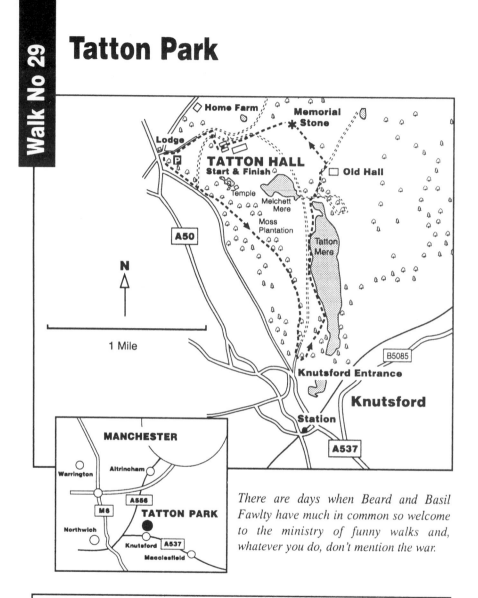

There are days when Beard and Basil Fawlty have much in common so welcome to the ministry of funny walks and, whatever you do, don't mention the war.

4 very easy miles which will entertain you for a couple of hours.

Route details in a booklet – Wartime Tatton available from the shop at Tatton Park. Details of opening hours and events from www.tattonpark.org.uk

There's a certain sort of walker who insists on getting kitted out with boots, rucksack, cagoule and walking poles even if his most daunting challenge of the day is going to be a high kerb in Bishop Auckland. For this walk in Tatton Park you won't need any special gear. In fact you'll look a prat if you wear it. This is a great walk to keep in reserve for the day when you're suffering from a bad back, haemorrhoids and a raging hangover.

Tatton Park, managed today by Cheshire County Council on behalf of The National Trust was, for centuries, the home of the powerful Egerton family. It was bought in 1598 by Sir Thomas Egerton who became Lord Chancellor of England. In its heyday the park extended to 25,000 acres. There are just 2,000 acres left surrounding the neo classical mansion designed by the architects Wyatt in the late eighteenth and early nineteenth centuries.

But our walk is into a more recent history. Between 1939 and 1945 Tatton Park was of national significance as the birthplace of Britain's Airborne Forces.

We're walking away from the grand house through a parkland of mature trees and rippling Meres, laid out it part by the landscape architect Humphrey Repton. But in the early 1940s these surroundings roared with the approach of aircraft and bustled with the comings and goings of soldiers and airmen.

An open expanse of park between shelter belts of trees was the DZ – the dropping zone. When the parachuting trials began trainees were flown in Whitley bombers from Ringway airport on the outskirts of Manchester to be dropped over Tatton. But eventually the drops were done from barrage balloons moored around the park. You can still see the metal rings fixed into concrete blocks that kept the balloons in place. Or at least kept most of them in place. One of them, affectionately known as Bessie, had a nasty habit of slipping her moorings and doing a runner. Once she got as far as Coventry before she was captured.

On the rising ground beyond the drop zone VIPs such as Winston

Churchill and General De Gaulle watched the parachute exercises. And there were famous names amongst the parachutists themselves. Evelyn Waugh as a secret agent of the Special Operations Executive, was trained to parachute here. On his first jump he broke his leg.

Walking on towards the Old Hall near Tatton Mere we cross the wartime airstrip. Wellingtons and Lysanders and Bothas would land here to be dispersed round the park and hidden under the trees. The extraordinarily wide bridge over a tiny stream near the Old Hall was to allow for the taxiing of bombers.

Just before we arrive back at the Mansion there's a scar across the field known as the Whitley Gap where a Whitley bomber with engine failure crash landed in 1943 and almost ended up in Mr Maurice Edgerton's drawing room. He was a sixty five year old eccentric millionaire who'd been encouraged to loan Tatton to the government to assist the war effort. His great love was big game hunting on his estates in Africa but, prevented by the war from travelling abroad, he got a rather different breed of excitement by allowing part of the park to be used as a decoy area where huge fires were lit to divert enemy bombing away from Manchester. Tin hats and tails.

Makes Basil Fawlty seem quite sane really.

An Amble to Warkworth

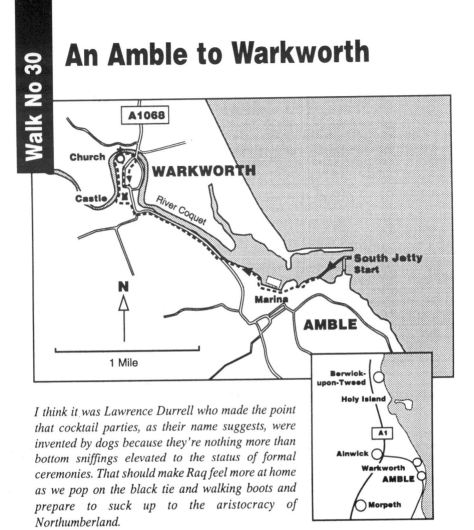

I think it was Lawrence Durrell who made the point that cocktail parties, as their name suggests, were invented by dogs because they're nothing more than bottom sniffings elevated to the status of formal ceremonies. That should make Raq feel more at home as we pop on the black tie and walking boots and prepare to suck up to the aristocracy of Northumberland.

3 easy miles which should take a little over two hours. There are bus services to take you back to Amble.

Route on OS Explorer 332 Alnwick and Amble starting at map reference NU273051 and finishing at map reference NU247061

On certain days of the year there's the option of taking a ferry across the river Coquet from Warkworth to visit The Hermitage – a chapel cut into the rock of the riverbank. Details from the English Heritage office at the castle.

As we stand on the rocky foreshore at Amble we'd better pretend that we're here to take the ozone cure because, as anyone with breeding knows, actually enjoying the seaside is what common people do. One could end up playing with buckets and spades and eating ice cream 99's with extra strawberry sauce and mixing with children suffering from tuberculosis or Sky Television if one's not frightfully careful.

And yet Amble is an uncommon place. There was once a plan to make it a great port – the Dover of the north – except that the powers that be apparently struggled to find Amble on the map so the plan was shelved.

Coquet Island, just off the harbour mouth, was to have been turned into a high security jail – the Dartmoor of the north – except they couldn't find Coquet Island on the map either so that plan hit the bin too.

So it was that Amble escaped from the burden of fame, fortune and Group 4 security (but then who hasn't escaped from Group 4?) to become the sleepy fishing port we visit today.

We set our course out of town along the River Coquet, its mud banks patterned by the barnacled skeletons of ancient ships and lighters.

But ahead of us and dominating the skyline there's commanding evidence that we're in the lands of the mighty Percy family who've managed to survive from the pages of Shakespeare's Henry IV to the age of the soap opera without much noticing the difference.

Warkworth Castle rears out of the coastal plain. The town around it, rising to the castle gates, looks more French than Northumbrian from this distance. It's a sort of Euro Disney in Northumberland, built as a stage set to glorify the Percy presence. The idea was that common visitors would be so overwhelmed by the splendour of the outer court that by the time they were admitted to The Percy Presence in the reception rooms of the keep they would be suitably cowed and compliant.

Unpalatable as this may sound to those of us brought up to believe that we're all equal in the eyes of Tony Blair it was actually a considerable improvement on the way things had been run in Warkworth before. As we approach the outskirts of the town we walk over a fortified bridge, rare in Britain and built in the 14th century to guard the place against Scottish incursion. Unfortunately it was built two hundred years too late. On the 13th of July 1174 (unlucky for some) Duncan, Earl of Fife who was part of an expeditionary force led by the Scottish king, William the Lion, took Warkworth and char grilled three hundred of its residents in the local church.

Two hundred and fifty eight years later the Percys took the place over and it was never troubled again. Except that a number of Percy Lords were imprisoned or executed for being Catholic, others had their estates confiscated for treason and the most famous of them all – Harry Hotspur – was captured at the battle of Otterburn and killed at the battle of Shrewsbury. None of these minor setbacks appear to have done them a great deal of harm. They still have their main castle at Alnwick and their estates in Northumberland and London. There may be more but I've obviously missed out on the gossip by not going to the right sort of cocktail parties.

Warkworth, which had been used for occasional family picnics, was offloaded to the State as soon as the Ministry of Works was prepared to take it in the 1920s. But business is business? And aristocracy is just a business like any other. Except that you have heraldic devices rather than letterheads. You may have been kicked out of the House of Lords but so long as you don't let your daughter marry some Australian Oik you should be able to make ends meet for another generation or two.

At this point a border terrier, frightened of losing his aristocratic Kennel Club status by mixing with the wrong sort of bearded Oik, was seen sidling out of the courtyard and whistling off down the river.

"If that's sucking up to the aristocracy I hate to think what he'd say if he was being critical", said he as he headed for the ferry to the Hermitage where he planned to say a small prayer for the soul of a common sinner.

A very common sinner.

The Roaches

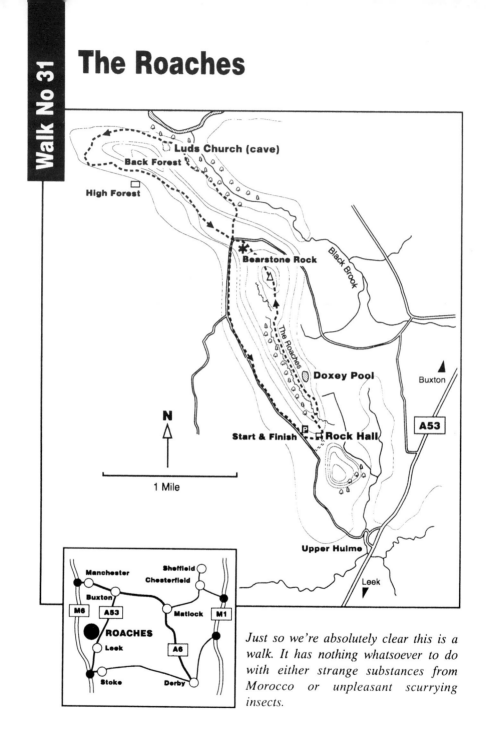

Just so we're absolutely clear this is a walk. It has nothing whatsoever to do with either strange substances from Morocco or unpleasant scurrying insects.

92

A 7 mile circular walk with a climb out to the Roaches summit and, in wet weather, a rather boggy walk out to Lud's Church. No longer than 4 hours.

Route details on Ordnance Survey Explorer 24 The Peak District White Peak area starting and finishing at map reference SK005622

The Roaches look as if they've been dropped in the wrong place. A towering and jagged pile of riven stone that must have fallen out of the giant's knapsack as he strode north across the Staffordshire Plain to make the mountains of Lakeland.

The principles of elementary geology were obviously never the bearded wonder's strong suit.

Our first glimpse of the Roaches Ridge and the craggy summit of Hen Cloud tagged onto the end of it was on a warm and hazy morning when they suddenly loomed grey blue out of the mists of the A53. As we drove closer they began to take on fantastical shapes. Occasional pulses of sunshine picked out eroded towers and impossible overhangs of rock. And all along the face deep chimneys of shadow interspersed a primitive chaos of precariously balanced rock.

We approach the foot of the climb by way of Rock Hall, a Hansel and Gretel confection built as the façade to a cave system that the owners of the Roaches Estate turned into a fanciful gamekeeper's house. Before the arrival of the fanciful gamekeeper the caves had apparently been the haunt of a strange religious sect that specialised in human torture. Obviously the forerunner of Alton Towers which is just down the road.

A stone stairway meanders up through the rocks to a wide ledge under the sheer main face of the cliffs. On the way we pass a rather incongruous overstuffed armchair carved out of the rock at the place where grand visitors to the Roaches used to hold their picnics. The future Queen Mary took her sandwiches here when she was staying as guest of the Earl of Shrewsbury at Alton Towers. In those days there were presumably rather fewer climbers to disturb the Princess's alfresco lunch. Today the faces of the Roaches are an ants nest of karabinered and belayed scramblers.

Once, though, visitors would have had to share the place with a different sort of hairy wild animal. The Roaches were fenced off and turned into a zoo for a while and it's said that some of the wallabies from that experiment have managed to breed and naturalise here and still live in remote corners of the Roaches plateau, having developed a penchant for crisps and sandwiches. We didn't see them but then they're probably frightened of border terriers.

The walk along the undulating summit opens up views of lesser, broken toothed ridges away to the east and, here and there, chasms down through the rocks of the western face from which helmeted heads occasionally appear in a most disconcerting way.

There's a long descent, first across open moor past the ruins of abandoned farms and then through a belt of mature woodland to bring us to a geological feature even more extraordinary than the Roaches themselves. The path is suddenly barred and beyond the railing the ground plunges away into a deep, dry ravine. A flight of twisting steps lead us through towering rock walls to the stony high altar of Lud's Church.

Sloping away from us there's a cathedral below ground and open to the sky, its only roof the reaching branches of birch trees that have a precarious root hold high on the cliff walls.

There's some dispute about why it's called Lud's Church. One version claims that there was a chap called Walter De Lud Auk – not so much a name, more an incipient anagram – who was the leader of a group of Lollards. They were religious dissenters who had to practice their illicit religion away from the prying eyes of officialdom. This hole in the ground was a perfect spot.

Another, more ironic, explanation for the name is that Luddites used to find sanctuary here after smashing up the new fangled silk looms at factories in Macclesfield and Leek.

But perhaps the most compelling explanation is older and more mysterious. The place has a strange presence. Perhaps this was a spiritual home of Lud the Celtic God of the sky – the same Lud after whom Ludgate Circus near St Paul's Cathedral in London is named.

In this remote and silent anteroom of the underworld the spirits of earth and water and sky would join in the fearsome turmoil of a Celtic dawn.

What's dawning on me is that I can smell the presence of Lud the rabbit.

To Green Crag

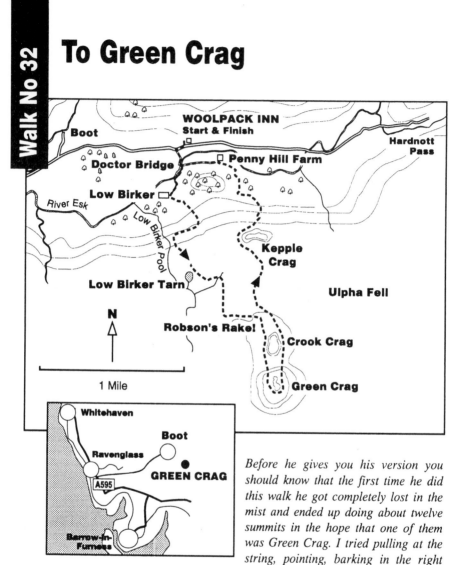

Before he gives you his version you should know that the first time he did this walk he got completely lost in the mist and ended up doing about twelve summits in the hope that one of them was Green Crag. I tried pulling at the string, pointing, barking in the right direction. I might as well have been talking to Napes Needle.

5 miles with about 1500 feet of ascent which will take 4 hours.

Route on Ordnance Survey Explorer OL 5 The English Lake District South Western area starting and finishing at map reference NY190010

Green Crag is one of those "I wonder what on earth that summit is" sort of mountains. It sits in the middle of one of the best views of Lakeland. It will appear as the star of tens of thousands of happy snaps taken by drivers on the winding road across Birker Moor. But back home when they're showing the photos to Auntie May they probably won't know what they've taken a picture of. Except that it's very pretty and rocky and you wouldn't get me up there if you paid me.

Green Crag is the last, southern outpost of fellwalking country on this part of the Lakeland rim. It soars 1600 feet above the Eskdale valley. (Actually 1602 feet if you refer to Alfred Wainwright's meticulous recording of measurement and, of course, it will be the final 2 that will ensure you're out of breath when you get to the top.)

It was a great morning when we set off, tramping out past Doctor Bridge over the River Esk, to Low Birker and the start of the ascent through a forest of juniper.

The light was clear and sharp as we zig zagged up the ancient peat track onto the plateau of Birker Fell.

There were clouds streaming in from the Irish Sea coast but Crook Crag was still sharply etched against the sky while we picked a route across a long, rising rake to a notch in the rocky wall just below the summit. We decided to name it Robson's Rake.

The panorama was becoming a little hazy but we could still marvel at a scene dominated by Harter Fell but with snapshots, too, of Pike O'Blisco in the Langdales and Haystacks peeping over Illgill Head. Bowfell and Scafell, Pillar and Yewbarrow descended into deepening shadow as we turned for the descent into the mires of Birker between Crook Crag and it's dominant neighbour Green Crag.

And then the lights went out. The cloud took no more than twenty seconds to obliterate Green Crag in its entirety from the landscape. Behind us Crook Crag had gone in thirty and it was as if the Eskdale Valley had never been. We knew where Green Crag had been a moment ago so headed in that direction. It didn't appear. The bogs became deeper. They were obviously in league with the weather. Out came the map and compass. Green Crag was north and east of us. Or perhaps not.

Now at this point I should say that this is a benign, if boggy bit of Lakeland. As we weren't on a summit we could scarcely fall off one and, having checked the map, we knew that we weren't going to hurtle off a cliff because there wasn't a cliff. What we didn't know was where we were.

For over an hour we picked our way through the mist, climbing to one high point after another in the vain hope that we'd be able to stick our heads above the cloud and see the lie of the land. We were about 12,000 feet too short. The dog was about 12,005 feet to short and about as much use as a chocolate fireguard when it came to route finding.

But not to be beaten we carefully picked our way from top to top. This one wasn't high enough to be Green Crag. The next one was too rounded. The third looked remarkably like Crook Crag where we'd already been.

And then, like the rising of a theatre curtain, the cloud lifted, a backdrop of the Eskdale Valley appeared and we found ourselves centre stage on Long Crag a quarter of a mile away from where we thought we were. Lakeland weather 1, Robson 0. But at least we got to Green Crag – eventually.

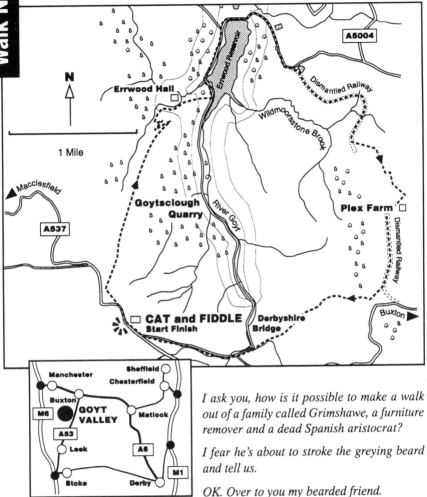

The Grimshaws of Goyt

Walk No 33

I ask you, how is it possible to make a walk out of a family called Grimshawe, a furniture remover and a dead Spanish aristocrat?

I fear he's about to stroke the greying beard and tell us.

OK. Over to you my bearded friend.

A fairly strenuous 8 mile walk taking 4 hours.

Route on Ordnance Survey Explorer 24 The Peak District White Peak area starting and finishing at map reference SK002718

99

It wasn't the most peaceful start to a day's walking. We were standing outside the Cat and Fiddle looking across a landscape of rolling summits grading through blue and purple to a gunmetal grey horizon. But we might as well have been at Silverstone. The air around us was blue, not with distance, but with petrol fumes, searing rubber and the jolly conversations of shaven heads above leather jackets emblazoned with skulls. Every few minutes a screaming, luminous wasp flew over the summit behind us and hurled itself through the snaking bends down to Buxton. This is the test track of choice for motorcyclists who obviously can't read the notice in the Cat and Fiddle public bar which says, bluntly, DRIVE LIKE A KNOB AND YOU'LL DIE. There's a list of those whose reading skills let them down in the last three years on the pub wall.

We headed over the hills to the sanctuary of the Goyt Valley. In a deeply cut and wooded glen overflowing with rhododendron and azalea there's a cemetery that will never contain a biker. It's the family resting place of the Grimshawes of Goyt. A peeling wooden sign tells us that the place was reinstated by the North West Water Authority. I suppose it's a small gesture of atonement on behalf of their predecessors – the water department of Stockport Borough Council who did their best to eradicate the Grimshawe memory when they built a reservoir in the valley. Below us, among the trees, are the ruins of Errwood Hall, demolished by Stockport because it might have been a pollution hazard.

The Grrrimshawes of Goyt. It rolls off the tongue like a name from the imagination of Charles Dickens. The Grimshawes were fabulously wealthy. They owned coal mines. They toured the world in their yacht Mariquita and brought back specimen plants from their travels to beautify their estates. By rights the Grimshawes ought to have been Gradgrinds. But they weren't. A staunchly Catholic family they were thought of as relatively benign landlords and employers. They built a school for their own children in which they also educated thirty poor children from the valley. It was run by a Spanish aristocrat, Miss Dolores de Bergrin, who died on a visit to Lourdes. The Grimshawes built a shrine to her memory on the slopes of Foxlow Edge above the hall.

A short stroll along the valley brings us to a tiny, rebuilt pack horse bridge, the only relic of the village of Goyt Bridge to survive the depradations of the Aldermen of Stockport. High above it are the faces of the Goytsclough quarry. It was here that the idea for one of Britain's best known companies was conceived. We're talking furniture removing. In 1670 a young man called Thomas Pickford had his estates confiscated by Cromwell. To make a crust he started taking stone out of this quarry to surface local roads. Eventually he realised that he could make more money by filling the packhorse panniers with other merchandise on the return journey. As people became more mobile, travelled to other areas to find work, he moved their furniture. The rest is history and not being able to find the potato peeler for the first six months in the your new house.

We're climbing out of the valley along a road with a gradient of 1 in 7. You may wonder why I'm bothering to mention it. Except that this road was once a railway. Goodness knows how many weeks ago on Walk 10 we were exploring what had been conceived as a canal but became Britain's steepest mainline rail route, the Cromford and High Peak, miles away near Matlock. And this is the northern end of that route – the Bunsall Incline. But even on a railway thought up by a madman this northern stretch was unsustainable. After a train delivered a bunch of passengers into the Goyt Valley rather faster than they'd planned and killed several of them the section north of Buxton was abandoned.

But the trackbed stretching away into the quiet hills makes for easy walking and we've three miles of moorland and majestic views before our next pitstop at the Cat and Fiddle.

At this point Raq spotted a distant mongrel and did a passable impersonation of a Suzuki 500 on a string.

The Mighty Caw

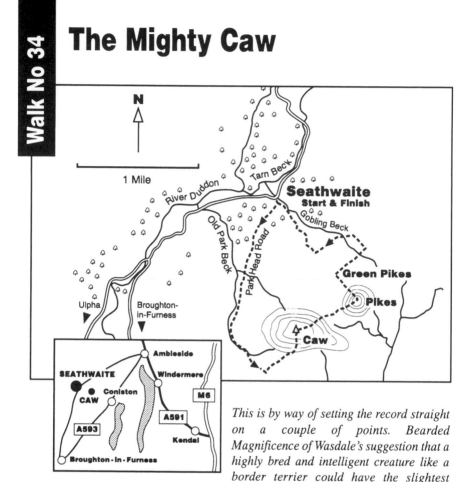

This is by way of setting the record straight on a couple of points. Bearded Magnificence of Wasdale's suggestion that a highly bred and intelligent creature like a border terrier could have the slightest interest in the mongrel classes is so obviously laughable that I felt no need to comment at the time. But since the walk in the Goyt Valley I've had a number of communications from the wrong sort of dog who were encouraged by his remarks. May I make it perfectly clear that I have no intention of jeopardising my Kennel Club status by any inappropriate contact. Also it's a Saluki, not a Suzuki.

A 4 mile circular walk with a stiff climb onto Caw. Depending on the out of puff factor it should take about 3 hours.

Route on Ordnance Survey Explorer 6 The English Lake District South Western area starting and finishing at map reference SD227960

We've got about 1500 feet of climbing to do today, my son, on one of the forgotten summits of Lakeland. Caw is a majestic chunk of rock, master of the craggy landscapes above Seathwaite. From the valley it looks bigger than it really is and that's a sensation that will recur on a number of occasions during the tough ascent.

But the walk starts gently enough, out along the Park Head Road which used to be an important commercial thoroughfare in the days when the quarries of Caw were in full swing. A mile out onto the fellside there's a walled and stony roadway that branches off to the left towards the quarry workings and offers a slightly easier route of ascent but we're feeling bolder and press on to where our track reaches the summit of the pass on its way to Broughton Mills. To the south west there are views towards the Duddon Estuary and Stickle Pike, a miniature Alpine mountain with a perfectly pointed summit worth visiting as day two of your weekend in this remote corner of Lakeland. In fact it was a toss up as to whether Caw or Stickle Pike would make the cut. Caw only won because we thought it was time you got seriously out of breath. Think of Stickle Pike as a gentler walk 41.

Caw has brooded over our left shoulder most of the way up the hill and it looms even harder as we turn into a little upland meadow of wild flowers that rolls out to the foot of the crags.

So few visitors come here that there's no clearly defined path on this side of the mountain. All you can do is pick a route through the mayhem of huge boulders that seem to be piled to the sky. You gain height fast. There's an exhilarating sense of space and air. Looking up you can see the summit. Just one more push will get you there. Except that when you crest the boulder field it's not the summit at all. There's another rise and another beyond that, each through rocks sparkling with yellow saxifrage.

But then you're on the top; on one of those high viewing platforms that many much bigger mountains fail to provide. Here the summit is sharp above steep supporting slopes and there are long, clear views down into the shadowy valleys of the Rivers Lickle and Duddon that snake around the feet of the mountain.

And then you lift your eyes to the horizon and are treated to a confection of peaks. Only two wedges of the great iced cake of Lakeland, to the south and west are devoid of summits. They're filled with the crumbs of little hills scattered away to the Duddon Estuary and through the Blawith Fells. The rest of the geological baking is in place from Black Combe to Seatallan, from Haycock to Great End, from Esk Pike to Walna Scar. Coffee and mountain cake will keep you here for a long time and even when you begin the descent towards Pikes half a mile to the north east the views will travel with you.

By the time you get to Green Pikes which are still at 1300 feet the long vista of the Duddon valley has closer competition, an extraordinary shatter of rock that looks like the remains of some megalithic palisade on the mountain.

A fell intake wall beckons back to the valley at Seathwaite 900 feet below. And on the reluctant descent I defy you not to be savouring the thought of sampling other portions of the hills that you've seen in the clear air on the summit of the mighty Caw.

Above the Breamish Valley

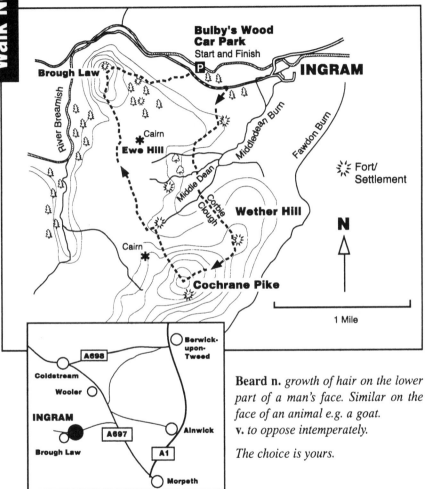

Bulby's Wood
Car Park
Start and Finish

INGRAM

Brough Law

River Breamish

Middledean Burn

Fawdon Burn

Cairn

Ewe Hill

Middle Dean

Corbie Clough

Wether Hill

Fort/
Settlement

N

Cairn

Cochrane Pike

1 Mile

Berwick-upon-Tweed

A698

Coldstream

Wooler

INGRAM

A697

Alnwick

Brough Law

A1

Morpeth

Beard n. *growth of hair on the lower part of a man's face. Similar on the face of an animal e.g. a goat.*
v. *to oppose intemperately.*

The choice is yours.

5 mile circular walk with a bit of vigorous climbing that will take about 3 hours.

Route on Ordnance Survey Explorer OL 16 The Cheviot Hills starting and finishing at map reference NU017163

It may only be a five mile walk but we've got eight thousand years to travel as we stroll out across the gentle slopes rising from the Breamish Valley. This was a land of wild goats and wilder men; a haven in the hills where families of hunter gatherers began to settle and become new fangled farmers. On the climb the hills around us are patterned with the score marks of Iron Age ploughs, shadows picked out by a low and watery sun.

We're walking through a pastoral landscape that was a defining moment. As population pressure drove nomadic peoples further north – as far north as the most remote islands of the Hebrides - in what we know as Northumberland they found empty, fertile valleys overlooked by hills that offered strategic defence. What made them settle here rather than move on in the tracks of herds of wild animals that provided a rich source of food is hard to say. But even in those remote times news travelled over vast distances. Information of ideas and husbandry methods would come with itinerant traders bartering seeds from the banks of the river Rhine and sheep from southern France.

It was an age of invention and dynamic change. By the bronze age they were creating agricultural implements that with minimal change remained in use in remote parts of Britain until the eighteenth century. They mastered the breeding of livestock and the care of crops that made these hillsides productive and sustainable places. Not that farming was an undisputed triumph. Archaeologists have found evidence that the early agricultural communities in landscapes like these were a lot less fit than the wanderers who'd preceded them. They died younger. They developed new diseases. But they stayed.

We've climbed out onto Wether Hill and are surrounded by the scattered remains of an Iron Age fort commanding a panorama of low, rolling tops and a pattern of oil seed and grain fields stretching away across the valley of Middledean Burn.

Cloud patterns chase across the saddle of rough, grassy upland that reaches out towards an even bigger fort in the middle distance. The slow approach to it brings its location alive and rolls back the millennia to a time when the master of Brough Law was lord of all he surveyed. A once commanding ring wall of stone still rises a yard high in parts. Stone that would have been carried up from a stream-torn gully perhaps three hundred feet below and built into a protective fortress within which there would have been round houses and livestock enclosures defended from the attentions of marauding animals and troublesome neighbours.

This Iron Age Des Res would have been a draughty billet but with one hell of a view from the bedroom window – if they'd had bedroom windows. And as we stroll back to the valley along a rocky stream side alive with flowering gorse we ponder the mystery. How did the primitive people of Brough Law manage to thrive up here on a hillside where modern agriculturalists can't do no better than run a sheep to the acre? Perhaps it's time to rework our definition of primitive.

Talking of which, said the creature on the string, before we head home I could have sworn you mentioned wild goats.

Yes, it's a shame we didn't see any wild goats when we were on the hill.

Apart from one bearded billy.

Budle Bay to Bamburgh

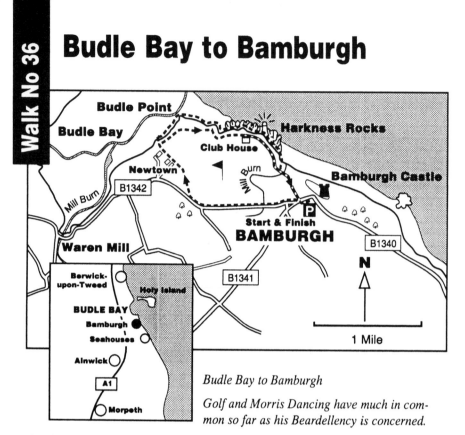

Budle Point
Budle Bay
Harkness Rocks
Club House
Newtown
Mill Burn
B1342
Bamburgh Castle
Mill Burn
Start & Finish
BAMBURGH
B1340
Waren Mill
Berwick-upon-Tweed
Holy Island
B1341
BUDLE BAY
Bamburgh
Seahouses
Alnwick
A1
Morpeth
N
1 Mile

Budle Bay to Bamburgh

Golf and Morris Dancing have much in common so far as his Beardellency is concerned.

1. They're obviously both a ritualistic cover for suppressed primitive urges.

2. They both encourage people to dress funny.

3. You wouldn't want your daughter to marry one.

4. If you know anyone who does both he needs help.

I think he must be going for the golfers' wives' vote.

A golf course at Much Thrashing in the Sand Dunes isn't the most inspirational place to start a walk – but if we don't do it who will?

A 3 mile coastal walk that will divert you for 2 hours

Route on Ordnance Survey Explorer 340 Holy Island and Bamburgh starting at map reference NU164350and finishing at map reference NU183350

We're strolling across the golf course to Budle Bay on a stunningly beautiful morning that's picking out the violent tartans and snarling dog tooth checks of the golfers' trousers in a most unappealing sort of way. But in a couple of hundred yards we've escaped from the clash of niblicks and the whistle of tormented balls to find ourselves on a deserted coast. Through tower blocks of sand we pass concrete gun emplacements still waiting in vain for the Second World War invasion force that never came.

They were built too late to protect these parts from the monstrous worm and loathsome toad that once terrorised the neighbourhood.

The story goes that a Princess from a local castle was turned into a worm by her jealous stepmother – well they have to do something to fill the long winter evenings in Northumbria. The worm slithered and slimed its way round the local villages nibbling at the locals who wrote to the Princess's brother, who was serving in the army overseas, telling him there was trouble at t'mill. He dashed home, landed at the pier in Budle Bay, kissed the worm (well he was a mercenary and had probably kissed worse) and turned it back into the Princess.

Are you keeping up?

He then went to the castle and squared up the stepmother by turning her into a loathsome toad. At which point everybody lived happily ever after. Local folklore's like that. Just as you're about to get to the juicy bit where the toad is given a wet slapper that turns her into the ruler of The Holy Roman Empire, everybody lives happily ever after which is just what you don't want to hear.

Anyhow, that loathsome toad is supposed to haunt these sand dunes to this very day waiting to be kissed by a border terrier. For more tosh about this coastline read any one of the four thousand or so books called something like Myths, Legends and Existentialism in Northumbria.

Reality's better. Over our shoulder Holy Island rises from a slate grey sea and to the east breakers roll in through the treacherous channels between the Farne Islands to break at the foot of its lonely lighthouse and thunder ashore on the long, sweeping beaches ahead of us.

Reality can be almost as strange as folklore. On this coast somebody called Ida the Flamebearer created one of the great Anglo Saxon Kingdoms and laid the foundation of an age of enlightenment that would shine as a beacon in Europe but which, unlike the toad and the much kissed Princess, didn't live happily ever after.

We walk out onto a rocky promontory with heavy seas tearing in all around us, history whispering on the wind. Because ahead of us is one of the greatest castles in England standing square to tide and time. Bamburgh appears as a castle of the imagination; of Princesses and fairytales. In reality it was a brutal and brutalised fortress on the frontline North Sea Coast. It was the first castle in England to be broken by artillery fire. For generations it slipped towards apparently irredeemable decay. Until the same Lord Armstrong who created Cragside near Rothbury poured a decade of armaments wealth into its restoration.

What we see as we walk along the beach towards it is a Victorian fiction. But it's a fiction so well accomplished that, as you scan its battlements and pick out its towers and high windmills, you'll imagine another, older Bamburgh.

You won't see the fearsome toad on this walk but you may well sense the ghost of The Flamebearer still looking out from the turrets of Bamburgh across the illuminated pages of history.

Bringing us back to earth the dog is of course more interested in the seabirds wheeling round the foreshore.

If I kissed one is there any chance that it might turn into an English Setter?

Lancashire Sea Fever

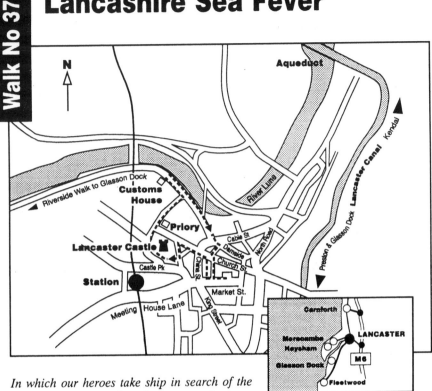

In which our heroes take ship in search of the age of sail and the salt and spice tang of strange ports in exotic lands. Sadly, a minor miscalculation of chart, navigation or positioning by the stars washes them up at Glasson Dock. The old sea dog is in mutinous mood and plans to set Captain Beard of the Blighty adrift in an open boat. "Avast landlubber."

Yes, that's a very good description of him.

An easy 8 mile walk to the sea which will take approximately 4 hours.

Route on Ordnance Survey Explorer 296 Lancaster, Morecambe and Fleetwood. The Lancaster section is available as a brochure from the city tourist information office.

Route starts at map reference SD496646 and finishes at SD445561

We're stepping out through a sun drenched morning across the grandiose Lune Aqueduct along the towpath of the Lancaster Canal. From here the city skyline is surmounted by two domineering buildings.

Lancaster Castle has a powerful history that may not excuse its domineering demeanour but certainly explains it – family connections with Henry Plantagenet and Henry IV and John O'Gaunt.

Dog touches forelock.

The other, even higher building (the domed and illuminated job that you can see from the M6) has less breeding. It was erected as a memorial to the wife of the Lancashire Industrialist, Lord Ashton who made a fortune out of lino. (To help anyone under 40, lino is short for linoleum which was the floor covering of choice for Government offices, hospital wards and members of the working class who had graduated beyond bare boards and could afford a week's holiday in Whitley Bay.) The architectural historian Pevsner described the florid Ashton Memorial as the finest in England – but to what?

Dog puts paws over eyes.

It may have been the Taj Mahal of Lancashire but it also celebrated the source of Lord Ashton's wealth. Poverty wages, brutalised workforce, children with no shoes so that the good Lord Ashton could live in the manner to which his labourers had allowed him to become accustomed. Sack them if they cut up rough, dear boy. Infant mortality, malnutrition – good for the soul, malnutrition, soup kitchens, pawnbrokers and the gods of the free market.

Dog looks around for a barricade to man.

Not finding one, of course, because the revolutionaries have all joined New Labour (where linoleum has been replaced by Yves St. Laurent shag pile), he tugs on the string in the hope of curtailing the babble and getting back to the walking.

In the interest of political impartiality – essential for all proper walking books - dog explains that the bearded bolshie can be forgiven because he's a member of no organised political party – he's a Tory.

Cheap gibe and only slightly less hurtful than suggesting membership of the Lib Dems.

As we walk away down the hill, the dog realises that we haven't offended the Democratic Unionists or Scottish Nationalists but they'll have to wait for another walk.

In the meantime, and dragging the conversation back to the sea and ships, we're strolling along the river in search of the lost Port of Lancaster. Lord Ashton's lino industry helped it to prosper. Merchantmen carrying jute from India and rubber from Malaya would once have tied up alongside the City Quay. We approach it across Lancaster's Millennium Bridge which we're told is supposed to be an echo of those days. Its twin steel pillars apparently look like the masts of ships moored in the river.

Dog blanches.

To me they look rather more like a monumental engineering V sign; another classic example of Millennium bridge-itis. But at least this one works. People can actually walk across it without getting sea sick. Except that if it's supposed to be a sailing ship this is the very bridge that ought to have made landlubbers throw up. Perhaps Lancaster should have had the one they built in London.

No matter. The City Quay today is part trendy housing and part derelict warehouses, a quiet promenade by the River Lune. Once it would have been a very different scene, alive with the winching and hauling of bulk cargoes – baulks of timber and bales of cotton, molasses and salt and stone. All spread across the waterfront under the perfectly proportioned classical facade of the Custom House. It's an architectural gem that still proudly proclaims an age of confidence and expansion.

Having walked into town we're heading out again, back on the towpath of the canal and making for the Lancaster's second port – how very grand to have two. It was built when the silting river was no longer capable of taking big enough ships up to the City Quay. The occasional narrow boat futters its way along the canal but we're walking faster. There are houseboats moored here and there, decks crammed with odds and sods – bicycles and window boxes, fishing rods and picnic tables. And then we're skirting the inner basin of Glasson Dock which is filled with sleek yachts and aged cruisers that appear to have had one rough crossing too many. Beyond them and through a bigger lock there's the commercial port, a bit down at heel and unbustling. There are cafes where once there would have been chandlers. But the merchant ships are still here; rusty coasters that have put into Glasson to unload mundane cargoes of agricultural fertiliser and timber. Exotic it isn't.

By the harbour side beard sits on a bollard and wistfully gazes out to the Lune Estuary and beyond to Zanzibar and the Coromandel Coast and the Spice Islands.

Dog lies down and dreams of chasing strange creatures in lands that he's never heard of.

Out of England

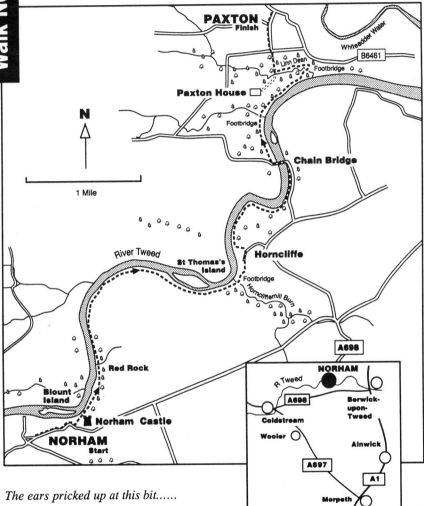

The ears pricked up at this bit......

"During the long years of border warfare a sight almost as fearsome as the approach of the Scottish forces, wailing and whooping like evil spirits, was the packs of vicious border cur dogs that scavenged the fields of battle and carried off what human remains they could find."

.......particularly when I told him that we were heading for one of the places on the border that had been in the thick of the Anglo Scottish wars.

We're on the southern bank of the slow flowing River Tweed at Norham which gets its name from having been the northern hamlet of the Palatinate of Durham. Just round a bend in the river is Norham Ford where Wardens of the English and Scottish East marches would meet to try to sort out the six hundred year crime wave that made this border one of the last places in Western Europe to be civilised. They generally failed because reiving had become the sport of choice for borderers English and borderers Scots. There was such jolly good clean fun to be had from cattle rustling and kidnap, theft and pillage. The odd murder tended to give the sport a bad name but it was generally played by honourable men who drew the line at torture. Unless it was really necessary.

We're standing in the long shadow of Norham castle which for centuries was harried by the Scots but lived to tell a rip roaring tale. Until 1513 when King James IV of Scotland decided to sort it out once and for all. He brought up a siege canon called Mons Meg, bombarded the castle for eight weeks and left it in need of some renovation as the estate agents would say. Nobody's been tempted so far. Under the castle walls a path meanders below the crags and through trees that throw a canopy of startling, iridescent green high above us. The river is a dour grey brown and so sluggish it's hard to tell which way it's flowing. In this landscape of perfect peace it's hard to conceive that once this was a land of broken men and scorched earth armies. The only people we've seen by the river today are occasional fly fishermen, the whistle of their cast complementing pulses of birdsong and their lines scarcely marking the surface of the water.

Long, sweeping bends lead us to the Chain Bridge and a foray into what was once enemy territory. On the Scottish side we're picking our way through a secret garden ablaze with wild flowers; the air heavy with the scent of wild garlic. We're exploring the spacious grounds of Paxton House where you'll have to pay a couple of quid for the privilege but don't, whatever you do, try to nick off without paying or the reiver's curse will get you.

Paxton House, built by the Hume family, is an example of the adaptability of the warring borderers. When the Union of the Crowns took much of the fun out of the sport of reiving they put the lance and steel bonnet in the cupboard, the pricker pony out to grass and took up another hobby instead – making serious money.

The Hume family had always been survivors. Despite the fact that they were constantly in bother with the Crown they controlled their patch of the Scottish border for centuries. They were particularly good at snatching pragmatic victory from the jaws of patriotic defeat. At the battle of Flodden in 1513 while Scotland was suffering the greatest military disaster in its history, Hume's Scottish Borderers were keeping out of the way of the fighting as much as possible and saving their energies for the altogether more profitable business of pillaging the dead.

But the money they made by nefarious means down the centuries left them ideally placed to enjoy later, gentler times to the full. Patrick Hume fell in love with the illegitimate daughter of Frederick The Great of Prussia and built Paxton House for her as a wedding present. The marriage never took place but we can enjoy the matrimonial masterpiece even if she didn't.

We walk out to the village past two somnolent lions so confident still of the power of the Humes that they scarcely bother to raise a stone eyelid to check on our passing.

And not a marauding pack of border cur dogs in sight.

Much to Raq's disgust.

The Hambleton Drove

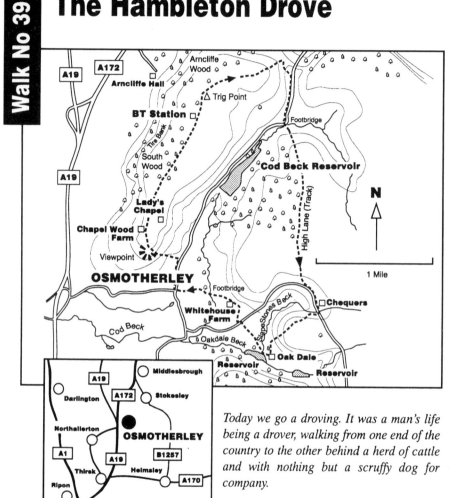

Today we go a droving. It was a man's life being a drover, walking from one end of the country to the other behind a herd of cattle and with nothing but a scruffy dog for company.

Put another way it was a dog's life walking from one end of the country to the other braving the hooves of a bunch of belligerent cattle and with nothing but an unwashed drover for company. But I fear we're still going a droving.

A 7 mile circular drove which will take about 4 hours.

Route on Ordnance Survey Explorer OL 26 North York Moors Western Area starting and finishing at map reference SE456972

In the good old days Osmotherley was a grand place to live. In the middle of the eighteenth century some of the locals starved to death because murrain, a sort of cattle plague, wiped out most of the livestock in the area.

150 years ago the villagers that didn't succumb to an outbreak of typhus starved during a succession of bad harvests. Pride of place in the village – somewhere between the open sewer and the plague pit was a hospital for consumptives.

Can you wonder that anyone who wanted to get past twenty five took to the open road? As indeed will we. But before we do, handkerchiefs over noses and sprigs of rosemary and garlic about our necks, we brave the village street to visit a little stone walled enclosure that's a direct link with the age of the drover. The Penfold – Pinfold is some places – was where stray cattle would be incarcerated by the local Constable until their owners paid the required fine. Many of them would have strayed from passing droves on their way from the great cattle breeding areas of Scotland to the London markets.

We walk out onto the Hambleton Road – a droving route across the hills - where once you would have seen herds of black cattle perhaps four or five hundred strong making their slow progress south. They'd be heading for cattle fairs at places like St. Faith's near Norwich where East Anglian farmers would buy them, fatten them on turnips and then sell them on at Smithfield Market. The drovers were hard men. To keep themselves warm at night they'd soak their blanket in a stream, wrap it round them and lie down in the lee of a stone wall. Their food was blood let from the cattle and mixed with onions and oatmeal.

But there were compensations. Up here on the hills the maverick drovers were free of the constraints that were beginning to hem in the lowlands – enclosure acts and toll roads. They had space. In their own way they were free spirits. They ambled eight or ten miles a day through the best of the landscape. Along the way they would have passed this entrance. Two gate stoups in the middle of nowhere which once led to Solomon's Temple, the home of another free spirit who'd turned his back on the modern world. The Temple was actually a hovel in which lived Matt Walker, hermit. Mothers in the village probably got their kids to bed by using the threat of Matt the hermit but, by all accounts, he was a contented and gentle soul who lived to the age of 90, distilled his own raw whisky and brewed his own beer. The thyme that he used to flavour it is still growing among the broken paving slabs.

We've walked on to Slapestones Ford and the sign of The Chequers. It's a tea room now but in droving days it was a boisterous meeting point for the itinerant cattlemen. It was renowned for its turf cakes and fine ales and a peat fire that, apparently, hadn't been extinguished for three hundred years. The pub sign read:

Be not in haste

Step in and taste

Ale tomorrow for nothing.

But for droving, tomorrow never came. They thought it would go on forever but the railways did for them. As we drop back into the valley it's in the company of the ghosts of a disappeared trade. Many drovers from Scotland and the north of England emigrated to new opportunities in the United States and it's said that they inaugurated the great cattle drives out of Texas. So I suppose we have them to blame for all those terrible B Features starring Mickey Rooney and Randolph Scott.

And Lassie.

Blucher's Drift

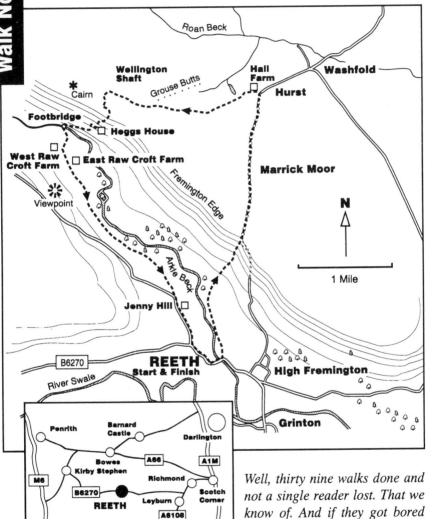

Well, thirty nine walks done and not a single reader lost. That we know of. And if they got bored after walk five they won't be reading this anyway so we can say whatever we like about them. A paragraph like this also keeps the critics happy. They always skip to the end to avoid having to read the whole book and will no doubt rise to our challenge and tell us exactly where they got bored and which walks were particularly *tedious. They'll also have missed the uncomplimentary references to critics on pages 14, 27, 33, 36, 41, 56 and at various other places in the book.*

Bristle is being oversensitive – something I never thought I'd say. In my opinion the review in Terrier Quarterly was particularly perceptive and the uncomplimentary references to bearded string holders in paragraphs 8,11,14,17 and 22 were entirely justified. On the princ le that ev n the most ea y goi re der can only take so much bol cks (sorry, the old word processor fault is back again) just lets get on with it.

Sorrreee.

A 6 mile circular walk lasting 3 or 4 hours.

Route on Ordnance Survey Explorer OL 30 Yorkshire Dales Northern and Central Areas starting and finishing at map reference SE038993

We're climbing out into the hills above Reeth where Swaledale and Arkengarthdale merge. We've been treated to a joyously sunny morning that's picking out a thousand different greens in the scatter of tiny fields below us. It's still cold and smoke from the chimneys of Reeth rises untroubled by even the slightest of breezes.

Reeth built its early prosperity on the wool trade. It flourished again as lead town but American technology eventually put paid to that when they discovered how to extract silver from lead ore. The price of lead fell and the mines and drifts in these hills just couldn't compete. Ironically on our climb out we pass a place called The White House, not quite as grand as the one in Pennsylvania Avenue but at least its occupants probably know where Africa is.

The great thing about this walk is that you get rid of all the feet of ascent at the start when you're fresh and fit as I was twenty odd years ago. As in so many things, from now on it's downhill all the way.

Dog pauses in mid stride.

When middle aged men start hinting at that sort of thing it's time to head for cover in the kennel because there's nothing more certain than that middle aged dogs will be dragged to the top of impossible summits just to prove that middle aged spread isn't really beginning to show and that middle aged, mid life crises are something that happens to somebody else.

We arrive at Wellington, a lead mine named after an Iron Duke in 1820 when the victory at Waterloo was still the definitive expression of British self confidence. The Wellington Drift gave access to the Blucher Vein, a productive seam of lead that took its name from the Prussian General who helped Wellington to his greatest victory. Scattered about on the surface there are still timbers and tub wheels and metal frames just as if the miners had popped out for a tea break and forgotten to come back for a hundred years.

For an hour or so we wander through this industrial graveyard. In the miners' spoil heaps there are fossils of creatures that went for their last stroll millions of years ago in the teeming waters of an Equatorial sea.

Sitting among the rocks as the sun cuts into the far horizon we look out across a rolling, changing countryside. Like all great landscapes it makes you feel very small and very impermanent.

So where do we go tomorrow?

A short walk to the printers.

Three videos of Raq and Boot 'Out of Town' walks are available

VOLUME ONE · NORTH EAST

Eric Robson and a slightly cantankerous border terrier on a string go walking in Northumberland, Berwickshire, Tyneside and County Durham. There are twenty relatively gentle walks in volume one in places ranging from Wallington to The Derwent Valley, Dunstanburgh to Durham and Keilder.

20 walks   100 Mins Approx.

VOLUME TWO · YORKSHIRE AND TEESSIDE

Our intrepid pair explore secret byways and discover hidden gems in eighteen walks that range from the Esk Valley to Teessmouth, Fountains Abbey and The Wainstones.

18 walks   90 Mins Approx.

VOLUME THREE · WEST AND CENTRAL

Raq and Boot (Raq's the one on a string) go exploring again in seventeen walks that range from Whitehaven to Lancaster, Kendal to Stanhope. As ever they bring you great scenery and easy to organise walks with a dash of folklore, history, humour and the occasional grumbles of a scruffy terrier.

17 walks   90 Mins Approx.

£10.99 Each
Available by ringing Freephone: 0800 027 25 27